GOMER SAYS HEY!

Inside the Manic and Much-Loved
Gomer Pyle, U.S.M.C.

By Denny Reese
Foreword by Ronnie Schell

Gomer Says Hey!
By Denny Reese
Copyright © 2020 Denny Reese
No part of this book may be reproduced in any form or by any means, electronic, mechanical, digital, photocopying, or recording, except for inclusion of a review, without permission in writing from the publisher or Author.
No copyright is claimed for the photos within this book. They are used for the purposes of publicity only.

Published in the USA by:

BearManor Media
4700 Millenia Blvd.
Suite 175 PMB 90497
Orlando, FL 32839
www.bearmanormedia.com

Paperback ISBN 978-1-62933-467-7
Case ISBN: 978-1-62933-468-4
BearManor Media, Orlando, Florida
Printed in the United States of America
Book design by Robbie Adkins, www.adkinsconsult.com
Cover photo resource Adobe Stock

Contents

Foreword vi
Introduction xii
(1) The Marine Way 1
(2) Television In the Sixties 8
(3) Gomer in Mayberry 15
(4) Pilot 22
(5) Season On 28
(6) Jim Nabors 38
(7) Season Two 48
(8) Frank Sutton 53
(9) Season Three `61 61
(10) Ronnie Schell 68
(11) Season Four 76
(12) Notable Others 83
(13) Season Five 100
(14) Variety Show 111
(15) Post-Pyle 118

This work is dedicated to the memory of Sheldon Leonard (1907-1997)—actor, director, writer and executive producer
Acknowledgments

There are many to thank for helping to make this book on the Gomer Pyle TV series a reality. It's difficult to remember back when I was stumbling around in the dark wondering if it would ever really be completed, and then the lightness of a wonderful Facebook group called Gomer Says Hey! That one I started in August, 2015 to very little fanfare—took off.

We started gaining members and they began sharing stories and memories of this show they had grown up with and had never forgotten.

Seeing all the love in our group gave me encouragement to go on.

I want to formally thank the following: Deonne Reese, Steve Barfield for opening up his home and museum to us, Teresa Barfield, the one and only Ronnie Schell, Greg Schell, William Pearson, Amy Jennings, Randy Turner, Craig Nystrom, Dave Monday, Joe Leatherman, Don Dapkus, Ben Ohmart for enthusiastically agreeing to publish it, Terrance Grundy of Editerry for meticulous editing, and all the gang at Camp Henderson.

A Special Thanks

I feel it is necessary to offer my special thanks to Terrance Grundy, a member of the Canadian Club of editors, and a highly efficient one at that. He guided me through this process with kindness and a love of all things Gomer, and kept me sane.

Terry, you are a one-of-a-kind friend. Whether we ever make a dime on this labor of love, to me does not matter. What matters is: We did it! And now future generations can read about and come to know the series as we do.

FOREWORD

Greetings! This is Ronnie Schell, and you may remember me from a wonderful series that ran on CBS for five seasons from 1964-1969, called *Gomer Pyle, U.S.M.C.* I hope you remember, because it was a hoot doing that series. It's also the subject of this book you are currently reading.

After reading this marvelous book and reminiscing about my time on the show, it brought back some of the greatest memories of my life. Speaking of my life, I can't remember a time when I wasn't being funny and trying to make others happy by doing so.

The key to being funny I have found is, if you do the research, most of your major comedians have had a tough time in life. I've never met a well-adjusted comedian. Due to the way they were raised or their life circumstances, they march to a different drummer.

I never set out to be a big star, and the way my career went, it worked out fine. I wanted to be loved and make people notice me and I found a way to do it through humor. This was from an early age. I started with a little pantomime group while still in high school. We played all the best places—social clubs like the Eagles and the V.F.W.

After high school, the Korean War was looming, and knowing my number was bound to come up, I joined the Air Force. It was the perfect opportunity for me to develop a comedy act, for I toured with the famed Airmen of Note out of Bolling Air Force Base in Washington D.C.

It opened a lot of doors for me. There are still a couple of bits I started out with long ago, that with updates, I still do today. On stage, performing, one quickly learns he or she is the center of attention, and given the type of personality who enjoys that attention, it is a tremendous high.

I laugh when I hear others ask (and they have), "Have you ever bombed?"

In my whole career I think I can remember two or three bad shows, and for the most part, maybe the audience wasn't with it or they were just off-nights. You just have to go on and not really dwell on it. Of course, too many off-nights, and a person might find themselves out of a job.

I played Vegas for over fifty years. I guess my time there included what is the heyday of the city that never sleeps. It was a swingin' time of Sinatra, Sammy Davis Jr., and so many others who brought the house down. I am lucky to have been a part of that era. I retired from Vegas performances in December 2018. I was feeling a bit tired and wanted to go out on a high note.

Now, a little about Duke Slater. This character that you saw every week was virtually me playing myself. Duke blossomed into Gomer's best friend. During the early stages, I'm not sure how the writers were thinking with him. He was kind of a Casanova, as witnessed in the episode "Gomer and the Dragon Lady." His amorous ambitions soon go flying across the barroom due to the prowess of Barbara Stuart.

My character, Duke, represented the audience. Frank Sutton and Jim Nabors were so over the top in their roles, absolutely "bigger than life itself," that they needed somebody to center the antics. You understand . . . a normal, sensible voice of reason, somebody who could look straight into the camera and say, "These guys are crazy!"

Frank came to the show with an impressive résumé. His dramatic skills had been proven in dozens of TV guest spots and he was highly recognized in the movie *Marty* with Ernest Borgnine. I don't think he ever got completely comfortable doing comedy, but he was extremely good at it.

I observed both he and Jim Nabors very closely; their work habits and the very environment was such a fulfilling learning experience.

Now, what about the *Good Morning World* environment? It was totally different. The show itself wasn't half bad, but we suffered some of the worst fates a TV show can suffer, and even in the Sixties, you had to almost begin hitting home runs out of the gate or your fate was sealed.

Number one: We had a terrible time slot. Up against *Tuesday Night at the Movies*—when first run theatrical films were being shown, we couldn't compete.

Number two: Joby Baker, my co-star, was a very formidable actor and a great guy, but he had a lot of trouble remembering lines. Had the show been renewed for a second season (which was highly unlikely) I don't think he would have been in the cast.

They wanted to replace him with another actor who went on to headline quite a few series—Bill Bixby. Since all of this was only speculation, we will never know how well a revamped *Good Morning World* would have played.

We might have even lured a few more viewers away from Cary Grant.

My return to *Gomer Pyle, U.S.M.C.* was a saving grace. It really was, and my favorite episode of the entire series has to be "Corporal Duke." Now Slater's character had changed somewhat. He had to be an ally for Vince. It was a more serious role to undertake, being pro-Carter, because Carter's character was still this supersensitive, uptight guy who always rails at Gomer—and the whole platoon for that matter—and I had to keep him from killing someone.

Plus, I had to shovel a lot of paperwork. And occasionally help nincompoops wrestle bronze boots off of swollen feet.

Looking back, these old TV shows, even some of those that weren't on long, were so well written. It's as if the writers had some extra sensory perception that they were writing for the ages. Someday these series will still play, and not a single soul involved in their creation will be among the living. But the shows themselves will live on. As long as there are new audiences to discover them, shows like *The Andy Griffith Show* and *Gomer Pyle, U.S.M.C.* will never leave the scene. The humor will never be old or offensive; our masterwork is forever frozen in time.

We were extremely popular in the Midwest and South, but surprisingly also played well in cities like New York and Los Angeles. Week after week, the Nielsen Ratings system proved it, and Fred Silverman, new vice president of programming at CBS, made one of the worst, if not *the* worst decision in television history when he axed all of the "rural" shows, or at least what he considered to be geared to hillbillies.

We're still being shown, and maybe we weren't "hip enough" for the early seventies, but none of us are surprised that more people remember us than remember Mr. Silverman.

Our variety show... Jim was such a multitalented guy, I think he just wanted to do something more than walk around saying "Goll-lee!" and "Shazam!" to Sergeant Carter all the time and creating problems as Gomer that he had to find intricate ways to get out of.

This isn't to say he didn't love *Gomer* and what it did for his career (because it made his career), but the last couple of seasons the producers had begun to let him sing on the show and use his real voice. Man, all anyone has to do is watch that one episode we did in Washington D.C. where he belts out "The Impossible Dream" to realize this guy was too big—too talented—to be stymied by weekly situation comedy.

So, he convinced CBS to give him a variety show. And he took me and Frank with him. Poor Frank found a new weakness in trying to do sketches. He worked hard and overcame a lot, but it was always a struggle, and in some close-ups, his nervousness shows.

I do know they were going to replace Frank had the variety show made it to a third season, but I also know that Jim, being the loyal friend he was, would not have let this happen. Yes, he would have walked away from a hit show for a friend. He was that kind of guy.

And we were a hit. We were the number one variety show for a while, even beating out *The Carol Burnett Show* many, many weeks—which was no small feat—but we were all friends, and of course, Jim later became a regular on Carol's long-running program.

I think Jim's talent was exploding around that time anyway. It was during the variety show (1969–1971) that we started going to Vegas. Jim wanted to go out and sing for the people and he took me along for his opening act.

And we played for standing room only, many, many times. Those were such fun and exciting times.

As for the others from the Pyle series, I remained close friends with Ted Bessell (Frankie Lombardi) up until his death. Early on, he got the chance to leave us and become Marlo Thomas' boyfriend on ABC's *That Girl*, and I don't blame him. It was a good gig and I would have accepted it myself. I also made a few episodes with her, playing an agent.

Roy Stuart, who was Corporal Boyle, bless his soul, was such a kind person. He was also very funny when given the chance to shine and he went on to some fantastic guest shots after *Gomer*, but died much too soon.

The way he left the series is bothersome for me personally, because when Duke returned, Boyle went bye-bye. But Roy never blamed me or anyone else for the way it worked out. He wasn't that kind of person. I think he was just grateful for the opportunity to be in the episodes he was (which were classics) and now he is always going to be remembered.

As most of you know, I even did a couple of episodes of *The Andy Griffith Show* for which to this day I am fondly remembered. That entire cast was such a seasoned ensemble, man, it was a pleasure to be in their company.

I find it truly amazing to think that we are on the verge of the show's sixtieth anniversary and it is still funnier than anything new being produced for television today. There is even a new movie, *Mayberry Man,* in the works that is going to be filmed in three places key to the whole Mayberry nostalgia craze—in Danville, Indiana (home of Mayberry in the Midwest), Mount Airy, North Carolina (annual Mayberry Days), and Los Angeles (where the original episodes were filmed).

Thank you for allowing me to be a part of your lives. Whether we grew up together or you are a newer fan, we are bonded by a mutual admiration of great series work.

I was asked to start attending reunions of *The Andy Griffith Show* a few years ago and I am loving every minute of it. Traveling across the country, meeting fans and making friends, I feel I have the best of two worlds. I am living in the present, but never far removed from my beloved past.

I plan to keep going as long as I'm able and there are people who want to hear what Ronnie Schell has to say about show business. My decisions over the years have panned out, and it is so nice for me because I never really had a back-up plan.

Maybe join the Marines?

Life is great and presents ample material. I've lived a long time, and the longer you live, the more material you get.

Ronnie Schell
December, 2019

INTRODUCTION

One might be prone to pose the question: why a book on the *Gomer Pyle, U.S.M.C.* (1964–1969) television series? Ask that of one of the knuckleheads in the platoon and they might very well reply, "Why not write that kinda book?"

It is time.

The passing of Jim Nabors and the much-anticipated return of the show to syndication, most notably on MeTV, has renewed interest. *Gomer Pyle, U.S.M.C.* has freshness and familiarity in equal measure.

Gomer says hey . . . and read on!

There have been numerous books written about *The Andy Griffith Show* (1960–1968), but research has failed to turn up any on the *Gomer Pyle* series. The country bumpkin with a heart of gold has remained in the shadows of its parent series. It is more than fair to call Gomer an integral part of the Griffith wheel. When his character was grandly written off to his own show in 1964, the departure was not as deeply felt as when Don Knotts left a year later. In Mayberry, Gomer was a one-dimensional character—funny, but limited nonetheless.

Having him leave the fillin' station to enlist in the Marines could have resulted in a major flop. Luckily for us, it didn't. Exceptional writers took the hayseed and slowly began making a man out of him. That they did this without him ever losing his country innocence or charm is yet more testament to their talent.

Gomer Pyle, U.S.M.C. is unique in that the show seemed to get better with each passing season. Added to the successful mix was the extraordinary choice of Frank Sutton to play Gunnery Sergeant Vincent Carter. The two played perfectly off one another. Watching the episodes in order, one can trace the progression from tough D.I. and raw recruit, to the mutual respect between two Marines that developed, until finally there was almost a role reversal. In one episode, there literally was!

Carter was insecure. He was all bravado to the boys, but one faux pas and his nervous laughter gave him away. Often, he needed Gomer to save him. Many have stated that Sgt. Carter over time becomes as big a buffoon as Deputy Fife. This writer doesn't think he ever reaches that level of ineptness, but he does come mighty close.

Frank Sutton as Sergeant Carter was all bravado to his boots.

Pyle was in some ways another Robert E. Lee Prewitt, a character created by Illinois writer James Jones in his blockbuster book *From Here to Eternity* (1951). Prewitt loves the army, but refuses to box, so every punishment they can think of is meted out to him. He remarks that, "Just because you love something doesn't mean it has to love you back."

Gomer Pyle couldn't be broken. Often it was he who broke the schemes and exposed the wicked ways of the city slickers. And he loved the Marines. The gullible private was a mystery, a marvel to behold, and an uneducated enigma to those around him. We as viewers—even those of us with no military experience—knew in real life he would not have lasted a week in boot camp.

This fact in itself made *Gomer Pyle, U.S.M.C.* somewhat of a fantasy. The 1960s were the era of the fantasy series. We will examine the

Sarge has the upper hand, for now . . . .

decade in the second chapter. Pyle fits right in with witches marrying into suburbia, genies in bottles, monsters living in haunted houses and thinking they are normal, talking horses, and talking cars.

It's doubtful some of these winners (and losers) could have been produced at any other time. *Gomer Pyle, U.S.M.C.*, though, actually could have been filmed during any decade. The idea had been used before, and it's been done and redone.

One of the first military sitcoms has a tie-in to *The Andy Griffith Show*. Andy Griffith had the starring role in *No Time for Sergeants* on Broadway and in the movie. It was subsequently made into a series starring Sammy Jackson and Harry Hickox. Ironically, though *No Time for Sergeants* (1964–1965) was well written and Jackson's character displayed more common sense, it was scheduled against the Griffith show on CBS. It was defeated, lasting only one season—due to the popularity of the actor who originated the role.

The chemistry between Jackson and Hickox failed as well. For they were not Nabors and Sutton.

In the 1980s, Goldie Hawn, a kooky and beautiful member of the *Laugh-In* (1967–1973) cast, had a hit movie called *Private Benjamin* (1980). She was sort of an updated, female Gomer. It was a thirty-nine-episode TV series running from April 6, 1981–January 10, 1983, starring Lorna Patterson as Judy Benjamin and Eileen Brennan reprising her role as Captain Doreen Lewis.

It is considered a modest failure.

The character "Forrest Gump" from the book by Winston Groom and follow-up movie has been compared to Gomer Pyle. There are similarities to be sure, although they are few and far between.

It is surprising no one has ever tried to revive *Gomer Pyle, U.S.M.C.* for modern times. As loyal as the diehard

Frank as Sarge, and Jim as Gomer, getting along famously for at least one scene (1967).

fan base's love for the show is, it is doubtful a new one would be taken to very kindly.

Gomer might say, "It's wrong, wrong, wrong!"

Gomer is still here; he hasn't gone anywhere. He is still creating unintentional havoc in all his dumbstruck pride. "Shazam!"

He lives forever in glorious reruns, tormenting his Sergeant Carter no end, and usually having to rescue him.

These two must have had a great friendship in real life. Indeed, when Nabors' series went off the air in 1969 and he wanted to headline his own comedy-variety series, he brought along co-stars Frank Sutton and Ronnie Schell.

The Jim Nabors Hour (1969–1971) was like having the old gang back together again. Except it wasn't. Nabors might have wanted his singing career to take him to new heights, but try as he might, he could not transform himself into another Dean Martin.

He became more known for making at least annual appearances on friend Carol Burnett's show. She called him her "good luck charm". Later he sang at the Indianapolis 500 race every Memorial Day weekend.

"Goll-lee!"

That boy from the fillin' station in Mayberry, with supposedly such little knowledge of cars, found himself singing and opening for the biggest race of them all.

This may not be a complete study of the series that many find exceptional. Many of those involved are gone and interviews are either impossible or near impossible to get. At its best, we hope this book can be a table-side companion to enhance your Gomer watching.

He's probably playing somewhere on a television screen near you. We love you Private Pyle. And we're rooting for you.

Denny Reese
February, 2018

(1)
THE MARINE WAY

"From the Halls of Montezuma to the Shores of Tripoli"

— "Marine's Hymn"

The Marines have a long-standing history of respect. They've been literally "first to fight" since their inception as Continental Marines on November 10, 1775. The original function was ship-to-ship fighting, providing shipboard security and assisting in land forces. At a moment's notice, the Marines are ready to go to any conflict that arises in the world. Why did Gomer Pyle's platoon never even leave the States?

"The Few, The Proud, The Marines," Jim Nabors (1967).

It is a question asked of viewers who are looking more at the big picture than entertainment value. The truth is, many of the extras in the show's opening were real Marines, as scenes were filmed on location with government permission. Jim Nabors lamented in more than one interview about how it bothered him to watch that opening sequence, knowing that these young men marching beside him were later sent to Vietnam, and a lot of them didn't come back.

Dissect each and every episode if you will. At no point is Vietnam ever mentioned. Pyle remains stateside, and his antics are played out in a rather safe environment. He is free from the hell that military personnel were going through in the sixties.

Gomer was inducted and went through basic training at Camp Wilson, North Carolina. After a few episodes, the action was moved to Camp Henderson, California, where it stayed until show's end.

Was Camp Henderson fictional? Most will tell you: yes. Thinking like a Marine, it's entirely possible the name derives from Archibald Henderson, the longest-serving commandant of the Marines Corps (1820–1859).

Called the "Grand old man of the Marine Corps," Henderson served an incredible fifty-three years of military service. He was one of six sons and fought in Indian campaigns in Florida and Georgia. During a war outbreak in the 1830s, he was known to have hung a sign on his door: "Gone to fight Indians. Will be back when the war is over."

Those familiar with the lyrics to the "Marine's Hymn" should know the places named come from real battles. In September, 1847, the battle of Chapultepec began when one hundred and twenty Marines stormed a castle being used as a Mexican academy. Breaking through this fortress was a monumental task accomplished only through vicious combat.

United States Marines marched victoriously through these walls—the Halls of Montezuma. "The Shores of Tripoli" line dates back to the early 1800s, when Thomas Jefferson was president and Marines fought pirates on the Barbary Coast. Gomer Pyle indeed joined a grand tradition of fighting souls!

Basic training. Ronnie Schell, forefront (1964).

The Vietnam era was one of the most difficult times for the marines and for the country. Tensions ran high as protesters and patriots clashed. Except for the evening news, television avoided the topic. Yes, Gomer would remain in the good old USA, stuck in perpetual training while war raged. Places like Da Nang, Hue, and Khe Sanh were never mentioned. There was never any backlash against the series. People understood it was comedy, therefore, it was appropriate for it to be removed from reality.

This is not to say that the entertainment industry has not at times tried to show the real side of Marine life.

The 1942 movie *To the Shores of Tripoli* starring John Payne, Randolph Scott, and Maureen O'Hara is a good example. Payne plays a playboy who enlists in the Marines on a lark. Scott is the tough gunnery sergeant, a friend of the young man's father. The usual hazing occurs, and the movie contains decent scenes of basic training.

The original ending was changed. The way it was initially written, Payne's character, through the help of a socialite girlfriend, is able to secure a cushy stateside job.

Pearl Harbor was bombed during post-production. The ending was quickly rewritten to have him reenlisting. All scenes of recruit training were filmed with permission at the Marine Corps Recruit Depot in San Diego.

One could reasonably expect films of the forties featuring Marines to be as patriotic as Mom's apple pie. One of the most iconic images of these kinds of films has to be of John Wayne from the beloved film *The Sands of Iwo Jima* (1949).

The United States Marine Corps has always been willing to cooperate in any filming as long as their beloved Corps is depicted in true colors, albeit their version of such.

Even those who have never served realize there are instances where Marine life has a dark side. Bad things happen. One such incident made headlines and reverberated through all branches of the service.

What came to be known as the Ribbon Creek Incident took place on the evening of April 8, 1956 at Parris Island. In a misguided effort to discipline his troops, Staff Sergeant Matthew McKeon, a junior drill instructor, marched them into a swamp—resulting in six deaths.

Originally charged with dereliction of duty, negligent homicide, and involuntary manslaughter, McKeon saw the charges reduced and was found guilty of the possession and use of alcohol along with negligent homicide.

Although the sergeant was not drinking at the time this tragedy happened, he had been drinking earlier in the day, as early as noon.

As McKeon's court martial began, the story attracted headlines and came to symbolize the brutality of Marine Corps training. Many of his fellow Marines took his side by saying such discipline is necessary to instill the fighting spirit in the men that they will need if ever in combat.

McKeon's supervisor, Staff Sergeant E.E. Huff, called him an "outstanding" drill instructor and noted night marches were a common formality at Parris Island. Huff went on to tell the court that discipline was so poor in the platoon that if he'd had the time, he would have marched the men into the swamp himself.

The defense team was led by a group of volunteer lawyers from New York City headed by Emile Zola Berman, who would later represent Sirhan Sirhan, assassin of Robert F. Kennedy.

The press had a field day demonizing to some extent the long list of military witnesses whom they said were biased and unlikely to turn on one of their own.

In came the most decorated Marine in history, General Lewis "Chesty" Puller. He described the deaths at Ribbon Creek as a "horrible accident" and declared the whole incident had been blown out of proportion. He also stated that a similar incident had happened in the army with ten soldiers dying, but no one was brought up on charges.

The final outcome resulted in three months in the brig for McKeon, a reduction in rank to a private, and a bad conduct discharge. After returning to active duty, he retired as a corporal in 1959 due to a bad back.

He later worked as Inspector of Standards in Massachusetts. In 1970, he gave an interview to *Newsweek* magazine confessing the lifelong guilt that had plagued him, and how he prayed every day for the dead recruits and for forgiveness.

Matthew McKeon died on Veteran's Day, 2003, at the age of 79.

Media coverage of the Ribbon Creek Incident had been heavy, and syndicated columnist Jim Bishop wrote extensively on it.

Even after the trial, Congress was persuaded to look into it. The Marines themselves wanted to shed the negative publicity and willingly agreed to cooperate fully in the making of the 1957 film *The D.I.* starring Jack Webb.

The project was already embedded with a touch of realism, having been written by Korean War veteran James Barrett about his time at Parris Island and based on his teleplay *Murder of a Sand Flea.* The film promised to show the truth behind the sometimes harsh tactics of Marine drill instructors.

Jack Webb was a meticulous Renaissance man who served as producer, director and star of *The D.I.* While his Sgt. Jim Moore was as tough as nails, great pains were taken to portray a character who neither cursed or struck those in his charge.

Jack Webb in The D.I. *(1957).*

Webb, of course, came to prominence first on radio, then on television in the ratings blockbuster *Dragnet*. The same elements held true with that series, as its head man oversaw every aspect of filming to ensure an accurate depiction of proper police procedure.

In *The D.I.*, Don Dubbins was the obstinate, prone-to-fail recruit, i.e. the "Gomer." The best scenes are the confrontations between he and Webb, who was determined to both break him and make him. Fairly new territory at the time, these scenes came to be clichéd and represented in countless future movie and TV military-themed subjects.

Here, in true Jack Webb fashion, was an inside look at Marine Corps boot camp.

The hard-hitting script jumps right in, and one has to wonder if Frank Sutton was watching and taking notes. Actually, although Jim Moore is comical at times with some of the lines he delivers, he is far scarier and more real than what we see from watching Sergeant Carter. The commanding officer is ready to throw in the towel on Private Owens (Dubbins) unless Moore can whip him into shape in three days' time.

Don Dubbins as obstinate recruit in The D.I.

With this scenario, Webb dominates the film from start to finish. He even finds time for romance in a subplot with a shop girl played by his future ex-wife and former Miss USA, Jackie Loughery.

Some sample lines:

"I'm not your mother!"

"I have told you people time and time again, your rifle is your best friend. You let it down and it will sure let you down."

"Tell me, Castro, did your mother have any children that lived?"

"There's a man hidden somewhere under that baby powder."

It might be more natural to assume R. Lee Ermey, who would play a similar gruff sergeant in *Full Metal Jacket* (1987) was indeed watching, for he delivers almost identical lines with a tad saltier language.

A *New York Times* reviewer said, "Against a colorfully detailed background of mercilessly thorough regimentation, the slender plot shows how an apparently soulless topkick scaldingly molds a confused recruit into a crack Marine."

He goes on to write: "Webb has staged a pounding graphic tribute to the Marines' training method from sunup to sundown, from the barracks into the field ... with the stage thus set for an offbeat drama, the star takes over and confines it to a rather one-dimensional close-up of a fairly monotonous fellow."

Sergeant Carter drilling the troops (1964).

Hopefully Jack Webb and that reviewer never crossed paths!

Today, boot camp is called "recruit training." It lasts for

thirteen weeks. It is longer than the training for any of the other branches of service. Successful recruits run three miles in twenty-eight minutes, do seventy or more crunches in two minutes, and seven pull-ups in thirty seconds. A typical day begins at 4 a.m. There is no privacy. Sunday is the only day of rest.

Watching Gomer Pyle with all the odds against him, complete boot camp and move on to more shenanigans in a few episodes, is encouraging. There is little doubt General Lucius Pyle was very proud.

What's that? There's no relation between Lucius and Gomer? Who knew other than Sheriff Andy Taylor?

Congratulations. If you have read this far you are now an honorary Marine for the duration of this book. March forward to read more about television in the sixties and the ins and outs of *Gomer Pyle, U.S.M.C.* and its stars.

"Goll-lee!"

(2)
TELEVISION IN THE SIXTIES

In 1961, Newton Minow was the Chairman of the FCC when he stepped up to the podium at a convention of broadcasters and delivered a somewhat controversial speech. He blasted television content, chiding those who produce programs to do better and ended with calling the medium a "vast wasteland."

Newt caused a lot of flak—and contrary to his beliefs—has been proven wrong time and time again. The sixties were a highly entertaining and exciting decade with explosive changes for us to watch right before our eyes.

It's true the fifties lived up to the title of "Golden Age," but this is not to say that the sixties didn't hold their own. Minow never took back the statement nor ever acknowledged he knew producer Sherwood Schwartz had named the doomed ship on *Gilligan's Island* (1964–1967) in his honor.

Newton Minow watching his "vast wasteland" (1961).

To say television came of age in the sixties would not be an understatement. John F. Kennedy, thirty-fifth president of the United States was as photogenic as a president can get. He and his beautiful wife Jackie enthralled the nation, and in 1962, she took them on a highly rated, televised tour of the White House. We watched with fascination the Kennedys: their lives, pursuits, children, and sadly, in 1963—death, as it came knocking in the streets of Dallas.

Much as Mayberry conjures up images of a simpler, happier time, so do memories of John Kennedy. Many of the producers, directors, writers and actors who worked to make *The Andy Griffith Show*, would go on to do the same with *Gomer Pyle, U.S.M.C.*

Sheldon Leonard had a proven track record when it came to producing hit television shows. He was the brains behind Danny Thomas' *Make Room for Daddy* (1953–1965) and Griffith's show, and would serve as executive producer on *Gomer Pyle, U.S.M.C.*

The series had eleven directors over its five-year run, the bulk being directed by John Rich and Coby Ruskin. Both had worked on *The Dick Van Dyke Show* (1961–1966). Rich went on to direct some classic *All in the Family* (1971–1979) episodes, and Ruskin's roots ran back to *The Colgate Comedy Hour* (1950–1955), with later work on *Sanford and Son* (1972–1977), *and* Here's Lucy (1968–1972).

The sixties started out with little to distinguish the decade from the flat fifties. Having been lambasted by Minow the spring before, each network tried to develop more quality programming for the 1961–1962 season. Among the shows debuting were *The Dick Van Dyke Show, The Defenders* (1961–1965), and medical dramas *Ben Casey* (1961–1966), *and Dr. Kildare* (1961–1966).

It seems TV shows were trying to match the sophistication of the couple in the White House. Even with this earnest effort to change the "wasteland," the top three programs were all Westerns—*Wagon Train* (1957–1965), *Bonanza* (1959–1973), *and Gunsmoke* (1955–1975) respectively.

The Andy Griffith Show was doing solidly in the ratings, the second most popular program in the land. The character of Gomer Pyle, bumbling and awkward gas station attendant, would be added the following season.

These were glory years for Mayberry. The show was blessed with an overabundance of talent. *The Andy Griffith Show* itself had been a back-door pilot, spinning off from a single episode of the *Danny Thomas Show* (aka *Make Room for Daddy*) and would spin off two of its own, with of course, *Gomer Pyle, U.SM.C.,* and *Mayberry RFD* (1968–1971).

Little did we know those tranquil and happy times would be so shattered by the events in Dallas, Texas on November 22, 1963. President John Kennedy's assassination in a motorcade traveling through the city sent shock waves through the nation, and every aspect of those four days—from assassination to the killing of the accused assassin to the funeral—was covered on the small screen.

Newsman Walter Cronkite who broke the news, interrupting the soap opera *As the World Turns* (1956–2010), has said it marks a time when "Television grew up."

The 1963–1964 TV season was already underway when Kennedy was killed, and any changes associated with it would not be seen until the next season.

1964 was the "Year of the Fantasy Series." Imagine if you will, what a magical, offbeat season it really was. We saw *Bewitched* (1964–1972), *The Addams Family* (1964–1966), *The Munsters* (1964–1966), *Gilligan's Island* (1964–1967), *The Man from U.N.C.L.E.* (1964–1968), and *My Living Doll* (1964–1965).

Cousin Itt (Felix Silla) from The Addams Family *(1965).*

With all of the harsh realism brought into our living rooms, America was ready for some escapism. Lest we forget—and the reason we are here sharing this book—1964 was also the "Year of the Hayseed Recruit," as Gomer graduated to his own series. In that the premise is slightly impossible, it can be considered both a fantasy and rural-based show.

Critics are often famous for being notoriously wrong. Glenn Herzer wrote in *TV Guide* on Oct. 10, 1964: "I don't think *Bewitched* will be-watched for very long."

Cleveland Amory called *The Man from U.N.C.L.E.* "a take-off that didn't come off."

Of *Branded* (1965–1966), six foot five-inch Chuck Connors' first effort since *The Rifleman* (1958–1963), Amory opined that the star was regularly beaten up by men who did not even come up to his elbows. (1)

What did the critics think of Gomer Pyle? Not much. Their opinion mattered not, for viewers loved him. Read what one person said by way of a review upon buying the complete series DVD release: "What a joy to discover Gomer Pyle after all of these years.

These shows take us back to a wonderful and better time for television. As a Marine, I can say life was not like this, but we loved the show anyway."

One fact abounds, while doing research, some pretty negative reviews were found from 1964, but there was never any occurrence of a bad word being said about co-star Frank Sutton. The man was a professional and extremely funny. But we already knew that didn't we?

Wonder how *Gomer Pyle, U.S.M.C.* fared in the ratings? It was Number Three in the overall Nielsen Ratings for the 1964–1965 season, with a score of 30.7.

ABC had its own military service sitcom, and it was so Gomer-like it was eerie. Not as eerie as *The Addams Family*, but that's another story.

No Time for Sergeants, starring Sammy Jackson and Harry Hickcox, was based on the movie starring Andy Griffith as a country bumpkin joining the air force. Producers had high hopes for it. Jackson won the lead by writing to Jack Warner and asking him to catch him in a *Maverick* (1957–1962) episode he had done. Warner did and was convinced.

Nick Adams and Andy Griffith in the finale scene from No Time for Sergeants *(1958).*

The main character, Will Stockdale, was a bumbler, but was loaded with common sense. Ironically, the show was defeated in large part by being scheduled against the very star who had originally starred in it, Andy Griffith.

There really was no time for sergeants when that familiar whistling began on CBS.

The series played as a smarter version of *Gomer Pyle, U.S.M.C.* Stockdale plays dumb to the hilt, but we are left to wonder how much of the dumb act is just that, and how much is real. A few episodes almost play out the same as the *Gomer Pyle* episode "The Survival Test," but these were sixties' staples.

There was one episode that drew praise from critics. "Two Aces in a Hole" was written with the Cold War nuclear scare clearly in mind, with pieces of *The Manchurian Candidate* (1962) thrown in.

Will and Ben go to a nightclub to see "Hip Hypnotist" Pat Collins and wind up getting post-hypnotic suggestions that have them thinking they are WWII bomber pilots.

Four comic books were spawned from the *No Time for Sergeants* series. Sammy Jackson's film work was sporadic, though he did star in *The Fastest Guitar Alive* (1967). By 1968 he had become a disc jockey, a job he excelled at, while continuing some acting here and there until his death from heart failure in 1995 at the age of 57.

Pandora Spocks (Elizabeth Montgomery) as Serena in "Serena Stops the Show," Bewitched (1970).

Flash back to 1967 and *Gomer Pyle, U.S.M.C.* was still holding at Number Three in the Nielsens—and, no surprise—*The Andy Griffith Show* was Number One.

In its last season, Pyle was Number Two right behind the new *Rowan and Martin's Laugh-In*. So ratings had nothing to do with Gomer's departure from the airwaves. There's no reason the series couldn't have gone on well into the seventies.

Several generational changes started happening in the mid-sixties, but watching TV in general would not reflect it much. The times may have been a-changin', but prime time wasn't.

Where was the counterculture?

Hippies and hints of revolution were around. Elements even made it to Camp Henderson. Most sitcoms played up the counterculture as a movement to be mocked rather than admitting its significance.

On *Family Affair* (1966–1971), Cissy dated a hippie or two, much to Uncle Bill's consternation, and *My Three Sons* (1960–1972) looked so fifties-ish, yet wasn't there an episode where Chip Douglas grows his hair long and refuses to cut it?

Sorry Uncle Charley.

The character of Serena on *Bewitched*, played by the alluring and mysterious Pandora Spocks, was definitely a hippie.

In the first episode of the revived *Dragnet* (1967) titled "The LSD Story," and featuring a character played by Michael Burns called Blue Boy, Jack Webb delivers a diatribe on the dangers of drug use. It was hilarious then. It is hilarious now.

How about the hippie sightings on *Gomer Pyle, U.S.M.C.*?

The biggest influence of the counterculture takes place in the last-season episode, "Flower Power" (April 11, 1969), with Rob Reiner as a character named Moondog.

Gomer encounters the hippies who paint flowers and peace signs on a Marine van. Jim Nabors also gets to sing "Blowin' in the Wind."

The summer of 1967 is known as "The Summer of Love." This is when thousands of hippies trekked to Haight-Ashbury in San Francisco for an extended love-in. Television had no choice but to at least acknowledge them.

Rob Reiner, Leigh French, and Christopher Ross as hippies in "Flower Power," Gomer Pyle, U.S.M.C. *(1969).*

Hippies make other appearances on *Gomer Pyle, U.S.M.C.* And guess who appears in each one? Yep. Rob Reiner.

Bill Pearson, a reliable Gomer Pyle fan, states the first appearance of a hippie on the show is at a wild party Colonel Gray's out-of-control daughter, Janice, drags her escort Gomer Pyle to. The hippie, looking more like a beatnik, is played by Reiner.

His other appearance comes in the first episode of 1967, as a potential recruit.

By 1969, eight years had passed since Newton Minow's infamous speech, and a new decade was looming. That fall, Camp Henderson was missing some familiar faces. In fact, Camp Henderson was missing.

Each decade of television entertainment leaves its mark, and the sixties can be classified as both swingin' and sensational.

Rural sitcoms survived into the seventies, but not for long. Soon the landscape would be dominated by sophisticated humor and biting political satire.

Gomer Pyle is immortal. We still have so much to learn from him. Gomer, we hardly knew ye.

(3)
GOMER IN MAYBERRY

If the incomparable Jim Nabors had remained a Mayberry fixture, never to be spun off into his own series, is it even arguable that he would have been just as memorable and immortal?

In careful observation of these early appearances by Gomer, it is easy to forget he was only in twenty-three episodes of *The Andy Griffith Show*. Added up, this amounts to less than a full season. These were spread out over two seasons, and he made his debut halfway through Season 3 and concluded with the final first-run episode of Season 4 which served as the pilot to *Gomer Pyle, U.S.M.C.*

We love our *Griffith* favorites so much, we tend to push to the backs of our minds each player's episode count. For example, Howard Morris (Ernest T. Bass, rock thrower extraordinaire) was only in six episodes, and in one he didn't even play his signature role.

Morris' fan base has remained fiercely loyal. So has Jim Nabors' to Gomer Pyle, but had things tilted a little the other way, it may have been a short-term role.

He first appears in "The Bank Job" (Dec. 24, 1962) as the rather poorly developed character of an employee from Wally's Fillin' Station, called in to free Deputy Fife from a bank vault he has carelessly locked himself in. The scene is really nothing to write home about. Gomer has only three lines. He doesn't even sound like the Gomer Pyle we all know and love, though there's a hint of it in the last line uttered.

Historian and Mayberry aficionado Randy Turner reports an interesting tidbit by telling us that "The Bank Job," while the first episode with Gomer to be aired, was not the first episode filmed with Jim Nabors.

That would be the fondly remembered "Man in a Hurry" (Jan. 14, 1963) airing three weeks later. In this gem, a harried businessman becomes stranded in lackadaisical Mayberry, where time stands still, mostly because two old women's feet fall asleep.

Jim Nabors as fillin' station attendant Gomer Pyle on The Andy Griffith Show *(1963).*

Gomer has some great lines in this one, including, "Good luck to you and yours." Toward episode's end, the look on Pyle's face is priceless when Malcolm Tucker berates the would-be mechanic, telling him the car is not fixed. We know, and Andy knows the car is fine. It's just that the man is no longer in a hurry. Mayberry's charms have rubbed off on him and he longs to stay another day.

Next episode, Gomer gets deputized for the first time by Barney. One has to wonder, even if the pickings were slim (and they were), why would by-the-book Fife want the inept Gomer by his side in times of peril?

A number of good reasons exist. It could be Gomer is such a goof that he will make even Barney look smart. Barney also likes to boss Gomer around. And finally, it is no secret that Gomer looks up to Barney, so having him serve as a deputy under him makes Barney feel that much more important.

Here is the Deputy Oath: "As a deputy of the county of Mayberry, I swear to uphold the laws and regulations therein, set to by statute 426 C, county rules and regulations, put there by this date, city of Mayberry, county of Mayberry, thereon."

"High Noon in Mayberry" (Jan. 21, 1963) is a clever take-off on the movie western *High Noon* (1952). It was written by Jim Fritzell and Everett Greenbaum. In the end, we find out recently released convict Luke Comstock is not after revenge as most everyone thought. All ends well except for Barney, Otis, and Gomer, who get "all tied up," literally.

In only his third episode, Gomer is still quite the boob, and yes, he does smarten up as things progress. Take into account that in the next episode, "The Great Fillin' Station Robbery" (Feb. 25, 1963),

Gomer doesn't know what a carburetor is. Yet just three episodes later, "Gomer, the Houseguest" (Nov. 4, 1963), he is so in demand for his mechanic skills, that former customers line up at night outside the Taylor house (Gomer's been fired and evicted by Wally) for advice.

"It's your shocks!" Gomer yells out the bedroom window, disturbing his hosts.

Gomer plays a key role in "Barney's First Car" (April 1, 1963). Despite his claim to always getting carsick on long car rides, "sick as a dog" Gomer's examination of the lemon Barney bought, helps determine that Barn is yet another victim of "Hubcaps" Lesch, played by Ellen Corby, later to play the grandmother on *The Waltons* (1971–1981).

She made ". . . three hundred easy clams from the sucker of the world."

Gomer gets deputized again in "The Big House" (May 6, 1963). Under the watchful eyes of he and Barney, two prisoners escape three separate times(!) In one scene, Gomer is on the roof when he accidentally drops and shatters Christmas lights, making the escapees believe he has a machine gun.

Don Knotts, Andy Griffith, and a duly deputized Jim on The Andy Griffith Show *(1963).*

Jim Nabors was in the process of earning his acting wings and has cited this episode as one of his favorites. He kept a still from "The Big House" in his possession for the remainder of his life to remind him of how Andy had given him important tips that helped drive his career.

Sample dialogue:
Gomer: "We better call the police."
Barney: "We are the police."
Gomer: "Shazam!"

Always remember, rule number one is: "Obey all rules!" This features a guest spot by future Oscar winner George Kennedy.

Don Knotts, Andy Griffith, and Jim Nabors get spooked by a portrait's eyeballs on The Andy Griffith Show *(1964).*

The October 7, 1963 episode of *The Andy Griffith Show* was a Halloween treat. Everyone in Mayberry knows the old Remshaw House is haunted. So, when Opie and his friend Arnold Winkler knock a baseball through the window, neither is too eager to retrieve it.

There's a lot of good creeps, chills and comedic interaction between Barney and Gomer in this one. Ultimately, the secret of the Remshaw House is solved.

While it would seem only right to spell the name of the haunted house as the "Rimshaw" House, our Mayberry authority Randy Turner assures us it is spelled "Remshaw" in the script.

Anyone thinking this inspired Don Knotts' first starring vehicle after leaving Griffith, *The Ghost and Mister Chicken* (1966), would be on the right track. In fact, Andy worked on it as a script doctor. It starred several Mayberry alumni, but alas, no Jim Nabors. He was super busy in 1966 keeping *Gomer Pyle, U.S.M.C.* a certified television hit.

Cuttin' a rug with Jim Nabors and Mary Grace Canfield on The Andy Griffith Show *(1963).*

Diehard fans are always happy to point out their favorite Gomer moments while he was a resident of

Mayberry. He fell fast asleep during a sermon of a visiting minister (David Lewis of *General Hospital* (1963–) on the topic: "What's your hurry?"

Gomer waited along with practically the whole town for the passing of a gold truck, and on another occasion, cut a rug with Thelma Lou's cousin Mary Grace Gossage (Mary Grace Canfield). She later became a Monroe brother on *Green Acres* (1965–1971). Yes, a brother to Friendly Freddy.

Was there a shining moment for Gomer in Mayberry? Well, placing consistently in the top ten of fans' lists of episodes is "Citizen's Arrest" (Dec. 16, 1963). It also contains Jim's favorite scene from the series for the way Barney impersonates him. Gomer turns the tables on him by showing him what's good for the goose is equally good for the gander. There are similarities here to the *Gomer Pyle, U.S.M.C.* Welsh rarebit episode, where a fed-up Gomer berates Carter. Only here, he does it to Barney while fully awake. It is in retaliation for the ticket the deputy wrote him earlier for making an illegal U-turn.

Gomer cries, "Cita-zen's Array-ast!"

Only eleven Gomer in Mayberry episodes remained. Had fans known at the beginning of 1964, they may have shared a common sadness, but the future was very bright for the spin-off that was at hand. Keen observers will see other similarities—to downright remakes—of Mayberry episodes to Gomer ones.

"Cita-zen's Array-ast!" The Andy Griffith Show *(1963).*

In "The Song Festers" (Feb. 24, 1964), Barney's off-key singing is disrupting the choir. Gomer saves the day with his marvelous singing voice. Watch the same scenario play out again in *Gomer Pyle, U.S.M.C.* Carter is disrupting the choir with his off-key singing and Gomer saves the day with his marvelous singing voice!

"Andy Saves Gomer" (March 16, 1964) is later replayed almost verbatim in *Gomer Pyle*'s "To Save a Life" (Jan. 31, 1969). Gomer

Jim easily passes the audition, with appreciative choir director John Masters (Olan Soule) and Andy on The Andy Griffith Show *(1964).*

uses his same disguise voice in *Andy Griffith*'s "A Deal is a Deal" (April 6, 1964), and again later in "Gomer Pyle, POW" (Dec. 24, 1965).

Possibly the strongest outing left before Gomer's enlistment was "Barney and Thelma Lou Phfft" (May 4, 1964). It was directed by the reliable Coby Ruskin who would go on to direct so many *Gomer Pyle, U.S.M.C.* episodes. Barney becomes too complacent in his relationship with good ol' reliable Thelma Lou (played by Betty Lynn). After all, he has a standing Tuesday night date with her every week. She uses gullible Gomer to make Barney jealous, and boy does it work!

When she kisses Gomer on the cheek, he believes they must get married. Cue in Andy to the rescue before things get even more out of hand—and it all ends on a happy note.

Most have a favorite Gomer in Mayberry moment or maybe

Thelma Lou gives Gomer a little sugar on The Andy Griffith Show *(1964).*

they all combine into one collective and happy memory. One thing is certain, every episode in which he appears is enhanced by his presence. Had the new show failed, do you think Jim Nabors as Gomer Pyle would have simply returned to his North Carolina backwater town? Would his character have been expanded? Would he have become the new deputy? Or would the actor have pursued other options, perhaps musicals?

It's all speculation of course, because *Gomer Pyle, U.S.M.C.* did become a smash hit. George Lindsey as Goober, Gomer's cousin, made a nice replacement, and *The Andy Griffith Show* remained a ratings hit despite Emmy winner Don Knotts leaving for a film career, and glorious Mayberry also survived going from a black and white town to a color one.

Let's just try to ignore those horrid green courthouse walls!

For twenty-three episodes, Jim Nabors, a novice, held his own against heavyweights. In both series, he was extremely lucky to have expert co-stars Don Knotts and Frank Sutton to play off. It's a shame Knotts and Sutton never shared screen time together. Would it not have been a hoot to see Carter getting his hair cut by nervous Floyd the barber, or as acting deputy try to squash the moonshining efforts of the Darling family?

Carter in Mayberry? Now that would have been a spin-off we could have rallied behind. It is easy enough to picture in our mind's eye these great performers carrying on, continuing to garner angelic laughs on that heavenly soundstage in the sky.

(4)
PILOT

Inconsistencies can be caught in pilots of many shows that were picked up by networks and had long runs. Sometimes these gaffes are simply not noticed at the time, or even if they are—time being the master that it is—does not make it feasible to go back and "fix" things. We must also remember that back in the day, no one realized that some pilots would be shown repeatedly until viewers knew them by heart.

Let's begin with the haircut. The scene opens the first official episode which is a ritualistic part of how basic begins. Why then, do we get the feeling that Gomer Pyle goes right into his Marine training without a haircut?

Because he does.

We must believe a few days of training have gone by from the pilot where Andy drops Gomer off to Season 1, episode 1, which is where the scene with the haircut occurs.

Sgt. Carter is putting Pyle through the paces and he looks to be a failure. Andy hangs around awhile in case Gomer does wash out. Even in 1964 during somewhat laxer times, a civilian would not likely have been able to hang around a military base, especially while basic training was underway!

The bases where Gomer was always stationed seemed to have incredible security gaps, except of course, when Pyle was on guard duty. Then even Carter had trouble getting past!

Plenty of folks, including Andy Taylor, are inclined to walk up to barracks windows, peer inside, and have conversations with Gomer.

"Be right with ya, Sarge!" Jim Nabors with Andy Griffith.

This scenario would not set well with the big brass or anyone who lies awake nights worrying about saboteurs.

One more item of concern is Andy being able to approach Sgt. Carter in the PX or commissary, and carry on a conversation. It is here he plants the seed—not to say Andy outright lies—that Gomer Pyle might be related to General Lucius Pyle.

Sheriff Taylor pulls a fast one on Sgt. Carter.

To any Marines out there having served in the early sixties, we ask: Was the PX off-limits to civilians or not?

It's time to stop fretting about holes in the pilot. The bottom line is, it was a funny episode and it worked to sell the series. There are many pilots filmed each season, including mid-season and summer season that not only do not sell, they never see any airtime.

Because a crew worked hard on these pilots, it is at least somewhat satisfactory when they are shown. Many never make it past the script stage.

Summer used to be an ideal time for networks to put together blocks of programming which often featured unsold pilots. Most of these aired one time and were shelved. They've never been heard from again, but wouldn't it be great if someone could rescue some of these gems and package them as a compilation DVD?

How many remember watching a pilot, liking it, and knowing nothing would ever come of it? With much of the lackluster fare we are subjected to as television grows worse, wouldn't it be a brainstorm to search through these ancient pilots for new ideas!

We're only dreaming . . . .

A lot of current pilots are not seen by the public. Back in the glory days, when so many million dollars were sunk into pilot films, packaging them as summer replacement series worked. These were

Big brass inspects the new boots. Pictured are: Frank Sutton, Frank Albertson, and Jim Nabors.

given titles like *Sneak Preview, Vacation Playhouse, Summer Fun, Westinghouse Preview,* and *Comedy Showcase.*

Vacation Playhouse replaced reruns of *Gomer Pyle, U.S.M.C.* during summer, 1965.

Would our keen readers enjoy taking a look at some of the pilots from 1964 that were competing with Gomer Pyle for pick-up? We thought you would.

Here are some doozies that aired on *Vacation Playhouse* from June 15–Sept. 14, 1964.

Hey Teacher! starred Dwayne Hickman as an elementary teacher. The plot revolved around a large snake being loosed upon the school.

Hooray for Hollywood had Herschel Bernardi as a movie mogul who doesn't see eye to eye with stars.

Papa GI featured Dan Daily as an army sergeant in Korea with two orphaned tagalongs who want him to adopt them.

Eve Arden starred in *He's All Yours,* managing a travel agency in London working with the owner's inept nephew.

Orson Bean filmed a pilot for a variety series called *The Bean Show.*

Love is a Lion's Roar had James Franciscus and Suzanne Pleshette in a situation comedy produced by Norman Lear, and originally titled *Band of Gold.* She played a French dancer determined to marry a handsome New York city bachelor equally determined not to get married.

The two had previously starred in the feature film *Youngblood Hawke* (1961). This pilot aired on the popular *General Electric Theater.*

Along the same lines, we had *The First Hundred Years,* in which Nick Adams and Joyce Bulifant attempt to make it as newlyweds trying to also finish college.

Perhaps the most intriguing pilot filmed for inclusion in the 1964 television season was an attempt to bring the Archie comics to the small screen. With legions of comic book fans and a previous successful radio run, a TV version with Archie Andrews and pals of Riverdale High was a big deal.

Or maybe not.

The full episode is available on YouTube as of this writing for any who want to check this out for themselves. The pilot features Jean Vander Pyl (yes, Wilma Flintstone herself) and Roland Winters, who was one of the Charlie Chans in the movie franchise. The plot involves the big school dance, and somehow, through a quirk of fate and possibly stupidity, Archie winds up with two dates—Veronica and Betty. The star, John Simpson, only has one other acting credit to his name, and that is as one of the zombies in George Romero's classic *Night of the Living Dead* (1968).

In 1976, ABC ran an Archie Comics special, a musical. It was meant as a pilot with decidedly more grown-up characters, and almost starred David Caruso as Archie. It reran in 1978. There was also a pilot in 1990. In 2017, a dark version of the strip called *Riverdale* hit The CW network.

One more Archie note—the *Archie Andrews* radio show ran from 1943–1953 with popular sixties' star Bob Hastings (Elroy Carpenter from *McHale's Navy*) as teen Archie.

Back to the Gomer pilot....

One scene that strikes the funny bone of most viewers is the bucket that Sarge places over Gomer's head, telling him to "Take a think under there." It is a bit humiliating, but a grand test which our Private Pyle passes with flying colors.

He doesn't see the stunt as an unjust punishment, but rather a move to make him a better Marine.

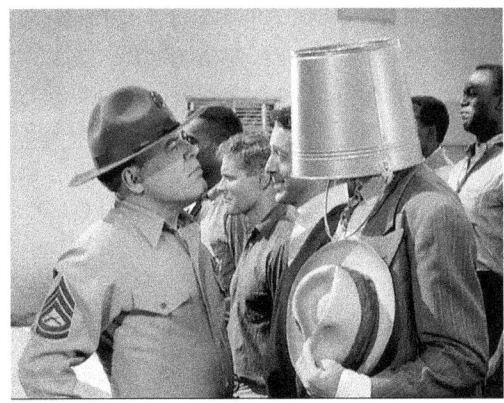

"Go ahead—take a think under there." Frank Sutton and Jim Nabors (wearing bucket) on The Andy Griffith Show.

Dress blues don't quite fit!

Personally, this writer would rate the scene in which Gomer puts on his sergeant's dress blues, as the single, best moment of antagonistic involvement between Nabors and Sutton.

The look on Carter's face is purely priceless. It speaks silent volumes.

Look fast for Alan Reed, Jr., son of Alan Reed (voice of Fred Flintstone), as a recruit. Reed is mostly known for his one other television role as beatnik Sheldon Epps on *The Beverly Hillbillies* (1962–1971).

Filmed at the Desilu Cahuaga lot, watch for a scene where Gomer is climbing a set of stairs. These stairs actually led to producer Sheldon Leonard's office. We know from experience, there are devoted fans who carefully watch the backgrounds in their favorite shows to see different locations being used again and again.

There may be no more an iconic location shoot for these sixties' series than Franklin Canyon. It is six hundred and five acres of public park situated in the Santa Monica mountains. The camera loved the lushness of this beautiful park.

It was here Clark Gable and Claudette Colbert filmed the hitchhiking scene from the Oscar-sweeping film *It Happened One Night* (1934).

The lake is the one on which Andy and Opie are skipping rocks in the opening of *The Andy Griffith Show*.

It is also the same lake from the Nickelodeon camp sitcom *Salute Your Shorts* (1991–1993).

Most of *Combat* (1962–1967) was filmed at Franklin Canyon, doubling for World War II Europe.

Again, it is the lagoon home of *The Creature from the Black Lagoon* (1954).

The list of films and TV shows filmed at Franklin Canyon is extensive. If only those trees could talk!

Go ahead, put on your bucket and take a think about that if you wish. We think we have properly prepared you for the next chapter which will begin *Gomer Pyle, U.S.M.C.*, the series, in earnest.

The pilot sold and Season 1 is about to begin.

More bucket time.

(5)
SEASON ONE

The very first season of *Gomer Pyle, U.S.M.C.* is the only one in glorious black and white. By 1965, most all network shows were in color, excluding a few holdouts. *F Troop* (1965–1967), the Western sitcom for example, began in black and white in 1965 and went to color in fall, 1966. The switch is partly blamed for the popular show's cancellation caused by the popular show's higher production values.

Gloomy, but atmospheric black and white fit the shows of the fifties where only a handful were in color—two being *The Adventures of Superman* (1952–1958) and *The Cisco Kid* (1950–1956).

Black and white also was a good fit for Gomer's boot camp days. There are a select few who don't care much for the early episodes. The series, like Pyle, is finding its footing on the obstacle course.

It doesn't take long. The very first episode, "Gomer Overcomes the Obstacle Course," sets the tone for the entire series and does so in excellent fashion.

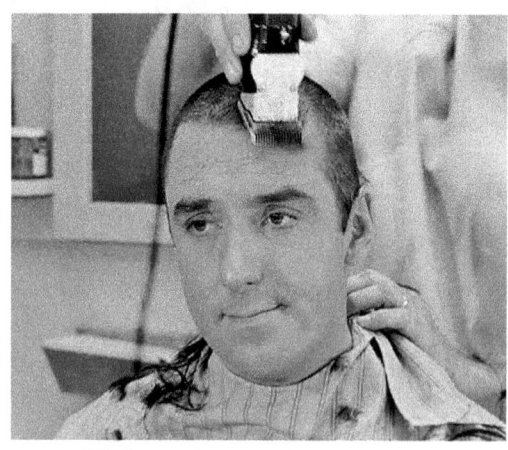

Haircut time.

It opens with the standard Marine haircut. There was no other way to film this scene other than film Jim Nabors while his hair was actually being cut. There would be no retakes.

Jim recalled many years later in an interview while watching this for the first time in fifty years to provide commentary for the official DVD release, he was shocked at the sight of his new look. He was so disturbed by his baldness that he nearly flubbed his line:

"Well, it ain't exactly the way Floyd the barber back home would cut it, but it is your first time."

Then we have scenes of basic training where Pyle tries to make a new friend in his tough drill instructor. It's important to note that while fellow cast member Ronnie Schell doesn't have much to do here, he is on board from show's start and ably works his way to playing the go-between for Pyle and Carter.

The real obstacle course at the San Diego training facility was used. Other scenes were filmed on a stage lot.

Carter has had three honor platoons and he aims to make it four. Gomer is likely to make this impossible as he fails at every test.

With Gomer winding up a tangled mess in rope climbing, Carter looks at him and says, "Pyle, what's the matter with you? I've got an eighty-year-old grandmother who can climb better than you!"

Pyle replies, "Well, bless her heart!"

There is authenticity in Sutton's delivery. He visited Marine bases and watched drill instructors barking orders. His army background must have also helped. He knows how to respond to every situation.

The obstacle course.

Wanting to please his sergeant and ensure he wins that fourth honor platoon, Gomer devises a plan to run the obstacle course at night, which exhausts him during the day.

Carter is sure he is goldbricking and is determined to prove it. This is classic Carter misinterprets what is going on and Gomer winds up being vindicated.

A colonel spies Pyle on the course at night, and after talking to him, the colonel is impressed at how Carter has inspired this man to want to pass the course.

After Carter finds out and sees a sleeping Pyle, he chides the others, "Knock it off and be quiet because this boy needs his rest."

Gomer does overcome the obstacle course. Vince takes a final dip in the water, sinking with a priceless scowl on his puss—leaving us knowing in no uncertain terms that the best is yet to come.

Season 1, episode 2 is titled "Guest in the Barracks." Hilarity ensues when Pyle sneaks one of the men's girlfriends onto the base to see him, a big no-no.

"Guest in the Barracks" (Oct. 2, 1964). Pictured are: Lois Roberts (Rosemary) with Joe E. Tata (Joey).

Sgt. Carter is ultimately dragged into getting the unauthorized person off base before anyone else finds out.

Joey Lombardi (who would later miraculously become Frankie Lombardi and a different actor) is played by Joe E. Tata. He would later go on to his most notable role as Nat, owner of the Peach Pit on *Beverly Hills 90210* (1990–2000).

"Private Ralph Skunk" shows us Pyle's affinity for animals. He even befriends one of nature's most feared foes—the skunk. His fondness for animals matches that of counterpart Elly Mae Clampett on *The Beverly Hillbillies*.

Any actor who can hold his own with animals and children is a good actor indeed. The great comedian W.C. Fields detested working with both and made some disparaging comments best not repeated here.

Gomer names the skunk "Ralph," because it reminds him of his Uncle Ralph.

Ralph figures into a subplot in which Sgt. Whipple (Buck Young) is trying to sabotage Carter's platoon.

There are so many good episodes in Season 1. As this book was being considered and ideas were being tossed around about how to write it all down into a concise volume, the original plan was to write comprehensive reviews for every episode. Spoilers and all.

For the sake of time and space, that will not be the case in *Gomer Says Hey!* Let us hit the highlights and perhaps review some that stand out it this writers' memory. A separate episode guide to be published later is not completely out of the question.

Is all that clear, knuckleheads? Good. Let's move on ....

"Captain Ironpants," Season 1, episode 4, is one of our favorites. It originally aired on Oct. 16, 1964 and guest-starred Pippa Scott who happened to be married to producer Lee Rich. He would later find fame with *The Rat Patrol* (1966 – 1968), *The Waltons* (1971–1981), and *Dallas* (1978–1991).

Here, Gomer works his charm on the cold fish of a Marine captain the men have dubbed "Captain Ironpants."

Jim Nabors and Pippa Scott in "Captain Ironpants" (Oct. 16, 1964).

Captain Martin is a no-nonsense type who becomes infuriated when Private Pyle tips his hat as she passes by instead of the traditional salute. This is how he was brought up to treat a lady.

When she assigns him a week of extra duty to teach him proper procedures, it is he who teaches her. He shows her how to feel like a female again.

We slowly watch her resolve break down under his influence, as we know it will. Captain Martin begins to embrace the lady in herself.

"Nice night for gas watching," Gomer says, reminiscing about how, back home, he and a honey would spend nights at the fillin' station, pour a little gas on the pavement and watch the moon reflect off it.

One won't find a lot of laughs in this episode. Frank Sutton as Carter has very little to do. It is fun to watch the dynamics emerge between Nabors and Scott.

Watch for Yvonne Lime as a secretary. She made her film debut in *The Searchers* (1956) and can be found in *Loving You* (1957) and *I Was a Teenage Werewolf* (1957).

She was married to producer Don Fedderson and later became a well-respected philanthropist.

In "Payday," Season 1, episode 6, the sergeant learns he should be more careful about what he says to Pyle. An offhand remark about goldbricking and slacking on the job causes Gomer to return a week's pay he doesn't feel he rightly earned.

While this is commendable, it is the military we're talking about. Ten dollars is ten dollars that must be accounted for. Refusing to take pay doesn't set well with the Pentagon. Yes, the Pentagon . . . .

Various attempts are made, but Gomer won't take back money he feels he didn't earn. Once again Sgt. Carter feels like he is about to lose his stripes because Gomer is doing the right thing.

He tries to trick a sleeping Gomer into signing a form stating he took the money.

"Write your name," Carter whispers.

Gomer does. He scribbles onto the piece of paper: "Your name."

There is a brief and very funny fantasy scene where Carter pictures himself right beside Pyle, scrubbing the general's floor.

There are so many tried-and-true sitcom devices on display during this successful first season. In "Survival of the Fattest," Episode 9, the survival test plot was also used in episodes of *F Troop* and *I Dream of Jeannie* (1965–1970).

Carter is buddied up with Pyle on a five-day survival test. He feels his know-how will be the key to coming out on top. Gomer outdoes the sarge every step of the way. There is a little bit of Davy Crockett in that boy!

In "A Date for the Colonel's Daughter," Episode 10, Colonel Harper needs a date for his daughter for the enlisted men's dance. When all the men he asks seem to be busy, wonder who he will prevail upon?

It's Gomer's first date on the show, and a reluctant one at that. He cannot get over the fact it is the colonel's daughter, and his heart keeps going "*ker thump, ker thump.*"

More of a worrywart than the colonel (Karl Swenson) is his wife (Joan Tompkins). To say she is a bit overprotective of "Miss Jane" is a vast understatement.

Things progress slowly, until while dancing, Gomer breaks into a jitterbug. The sight seems a little shocking to those at the dance.

After the couple sneaks off, the parents fear the worst. But they should have watched a few previous episodes and put those fears aside. After all, their daughter is out with the safest Marine on base. The safest Marine ever—Gomer Pyle.

Karl Swenson is best known for playing mill owner Lars Hanson on *Little House on the Prairie* from 1974–1978. He and Joan Tompkins were married in real life.

In this episode, we learn that Gomer, like Barney Fife, once bought his parents a septic tank for a present.

Jumping to the eighth episode of the first season, we find some notable firsts.

"Gomer and the Dragon Lady" is a winner. Barbara Stuart makes her first appearance, but she is not playing the role of Carter's long-suffering girlfriend Bunny here.

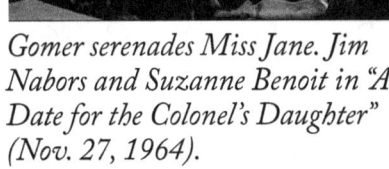

Gomer serenades Miss Jane. Jim Nabors and Suzanne Benoit in "A Date for the Colonel's Daughter" (Nov. 27, 1964).

Stuart plays Hannah Troy, owner of a rough bar the Marines frequent, and she is known by the tough moniker "Dragon Lady."

She can hold her own against any rowdy drunk, throwing them clear across the room, making them sorry they messed with her.

Sgt. Carter is again embarrassed in front of the men; mostly he blames Gomer. When a lieutenant (played by David Frankham) chastises him, Carter vows to get even with Pyle.

"I'd love to see Pyle get thrown across the room," Carter says.

He devises a plan, a contest rigged for Gomer to win. He tells him it is tradition, knowing the recruit wants to uphold Marine traditions. The winner of the contest is to go up to the Dragon Lady and say, "Dragon Lady, I'm here for my first liberty kiss."

Gomer doesn't feel right about kissing a total stranger, tradition or not. He would rather go see a Ma and Pa Kettle movie. Enter

Duke Slater (Ronnie Schell in a stand-out performance) who offers to be Gomer's proxy.

Barbara Stuart's first appearance, as Hannah Troy aka The Dragon Lady, with Frank Sutton in "Gomer and the Dragon Lady" (Nov. 13, 1964).

We know this is not going to end well for Duke, who calls himself "L.B." (Lover Boy) and promptly feels the Dragon Lady's wrath.

Carter sends some of the boys to find Gomer and bring him to the bar, somehow, someway.

Once Gomer arrives, Carter lays it on thick about how the tradition is finally going to be broken. Not wanting to disappoint his beloved sergeant, Gomer finally agrees to the kiss.

The payoff is wonderful. Notice the look on Gomer's face and the one on poor old Vince Carter as well, knowing he has been one-upped again.

Before we leave Season 1—and we're only two months into it—let's look at two more top episodes.

"The Case of the Marine Bandit," Episode 13, is more fun than watching hand silhouettes on the wall.

Author Anthony Liccione once wrote, "It seems it doesn't pay to be good anymore, especially when people are short-changing you for evil."

Had Gomer Pyle or even Vince Carter ever heard these words, it might have saved both some grief. The two stop to help damsel in distress, Betty Ann, whose car has broken down.

"Problem starts with an S," Pyle says, beaming. "Wanna guess what it is?"

No one wants to guess. It is a spark plug, and the private simply replaces it. He can't figure out how it would just pop off like that.

Given Gomer is the one who "fixed" her car, and she can only ride one, Carter is left to shake his head in disgust. She takes Gomer home to Mother.

He is smitten with the nice, cozy family scene. The little old lady, played by Ellen Corby, needs cooking sherry to complete her dinner.

Betty Ann drives Gomer to the "Spirits Store," where he is to hand the man a note. Little does he know he is robbing the place!

He is classified as the Marine Bandit.

Later on that evening in the parlor, Betty Ann asks him what he used to do when alone with a girl back home. It is then he pulls down the shade and shows her the shadowy hand silhouettes.

Afterward, Carter manages to push Pyle out of the way for another date by making him stay on base to clean. He goes to meet Betty Ann and Mom and also unwittingly helps in a robbery.

Carter puts it together while listening to a radio broadcast about the Marine Bandit, but it is a little too late. Gomer once again saves the day. He too has heard the same broadcast and brings the cops on the scene.

"Makin' silhouettes on the wall— that don't bother me at all!" Jim Nabors with Kathie Browne in "The Case of the Marine Bandit" (Dec. 18, 1964).

The ending of this is a real kicker. Watch for yourselves.

Now for this author's favorite first-season half hour. It is "Sergeant of the Week," Episode 14.

A sitcom staple is the case of mistaken identity. Carter is highly upset at being passed over for the honor of "Sergeant of the Week," so he is riding his men hard.

Pyle, who is usually the bane of Carter's existence, is sidelined with a bad cold. Through the normal channels of sitcom misunderstandings, Carter comes to believe Pyle is dying.

"Someone's been riding him too hard," Lt. Ames tells him. "Sooner or later this happens."

Contrary to what Carter believes, the lieutenant is speaking about a horse. The medical reports were mixed up. Imagine that!

Convinced Gomer is on his way out, Carter wants to make his last days comfortable. Per doctor's orders, he takes the patient an apple, sugar cubes, and a fly swatter to keep the flies away.

At one point it appears Gomer is going into convulsions. He is really listening via earphone to rock 'n' roll music on a transistor radio.

Gomer, usually seen having a brush with his sarge, is this time receiving one! Sutton attends to Nabors in "Sergeant of the Week" (Dec. 25, 1964.)

Within the allotted time, Carter realizes his mistake. Before he can wrongfully explode onto Pyle, he is called before the colonel. Because of his "unwavering love and devotion to a dumb animal" (the dying horse), Sgt. Vincent Carter is awarded "Sergeant of the Week."

Closing quote: "Gomer; call me Gomer."

Some other first-season moments include Gomer, as MP, marching a government investigator off to the brig, Gomer capturing a gang of thieves robbing a Marine warehouse, double dating with the Sarge, writing fake love letters from an admirer to Sgt. Carter, and taking a downtown trip that somehow accidentally has him winding up in Rome, Italy.

Among the first-season guest stars, we find Don Rickles as an old war buddy of Carter's, Robert Emhardt who was the "Man in a Hurry" on *The Andy Griffith Show*, and Frank Parker (Shawn Brady from the soap opera *Days of our Lives*) as a bully in "Gomer Learns a Bully," Episode 5. Karen Sharpe and Suzanne Benoit feature brightly, and then there is James Hampton (Dobbs from *F Troop*) as a Marine from a feuding family back in Gomer's neck of the woods, Norris Goff (from radio's *Lum and Abner* series) as Grandpa Pyle, as well as Ken Lynch and Gavin MacLeod.

There are many things about Season 1 of *Gomer Pyle, U.S.M.C.* for which we are grateful. We are glad Sgt. Carter's farewell to the troops wasn't definite.

We are pleasantly surprised that upon graduation, Pyle and gang end up back with Carter at Camp Henderson in California.

It's good to see Forrest Compton come into play as the gruff, but sometimes genial Colonel Gray.

And to just watch the coming together, all elements falling into place of what is destined to be one of the best sitcoms of the sixties decade.

Glad you made it Private Pyle. It took a lot of determination and good old gumption, but Season 1 was a success.

Four more years would follow.

(6)
JIM NABORS

He sure is a handsome Gomer!

The small town of Sylcauga, Alabama, in which James Thurston Nabors was born and raised, was more Mayberry than Mayberry was. His father Fred was the town constable and could aptly be described as closer in personage to Sheriff Andy Taylor than Andy Griffith. Fred used common sense and down-home psychology in dealing with people, often driving lawbreakers home with a simple admonishment.

Mother Mavis worked at an all-night truck stop. Both parents made sure young Jimmy and his two sisters had a secure family life. He was a sickly child from birth, weakened by asthma, and for a time it was believed he would not reach adulthood.

He was blessed with a vivid imagination and loved going to the movies. Jim especially loved musicals. His first display of talent was taking up the clarinet in the school band. He also loved to dance the jitterbug, which because of his gangly size was a sight to see. He won several dance contests.

After graduating high school, he entered the University of Alabama to study business. Jim's studying would prove to be a boon years later when he began investing his *Gomer Pyle* profits into real estate.

Jim's devotion to his alma mater remained strong, and he was a huge fan of the Crimson Tide. At the news of his passing, author Winston Groom (*Forrest Gump*) recalled a story from 1966 when

Nabors was scheduled to appear in Tuscaloosa for Homecoming festivities.

"D.R. Jordan was the Homecoming Committee chairman in '66 and was having difficulty getting Nabors, after his L.A. flight to Atlanta then Tuscaloosa for his Friday-night homecoming appearance. He went to UA President Dr. Frank Rose, asking him to pick him up in Atlanta. Dr. Rose told D. R. he would have to ask Coach Bryant, as the athletic department had the final say-so on the plane's use.

"Let me entertain you!" Jim with Jerry Van Dyke in their Gomer Pyle *nightclub act.*

"D.R. went to see Coach Bryant and asked him if the Homecoming Committee could use the plane to pick up Jim Nabors in Atlanta. Coach Bryant responded typically, 'Who in the hell is Jim Nabors?'

"D.R. quickly explained that he played Gomer Pyle on TV.

"Coach Bryant grinned and answered, 'Hell, that's the only TV show me and Mary Harmon watch. Take the plane and go get him!'"

While in college, besides a love of dancing, another bug bit when Jim fell head over hills with entertaining others. Along with college buddy Jimmy Pursell, Nabors would visit Phoenix City, aka Sin City, known for its raunchy nightclubs and strip joints.

Soon the none-too-shy Alabama boy found himself center stage. He developed an act that he would perform for the rest of his life. It was

The essence of Gomer's character: dumbfounded but deep!

a combination of a dumb country boy dumbfounded by life and circumstances, offset by his singing operatics.

The double-sided act was different enough to attract many fans. Jim somehow found a way to make this work.

In 1954, Jim journeyed to the big city, as in New York City. He had an eye on Broadway. He found a day job at as a secretary at the United Nations. Jim was deathly sick the entire time there. His asthma had returned.

He soon left New York City for the sake of self-preservation and worked briefly as a film editor for a TV station in Chattanooga. Friends advised him of the wise old adage "Go West Young Man," and he did just that.

About this move, he later told NBC's Matt Lauer in an interview, "From the time I really started to experience that dry air, somewhere around Arizona, something miraculous happened for the first time in my life. I could breathe. Without great effort."

Throughout the fifties, entertaining was foremost on the agenda. He continued to perfect his night club act at a Santa Monica club where he first met fellow comedian Ronnie Schell.

Schell marveled at the young man's act and told him he didn't quite know what he did, but he was very good at it. It was the beginning of a lifelong friendship.

It was a place called The Horn. Fate would have it that one night, none other than Andy Griffith himself came inside and sat in the audience for one of Jim's performances. He immediately made contact and told him that if he ever found a part for him on his CBS television program, he would be in touch.

Jim didn't know what to make of this. He had been on *The Steve Allen Show*, but Andy's show was watched by millions. It was the chance of a lifetime.

It didn't take long for Andy to convince the production staff, and he came calling again. It is no cliché to say "the rest is history."

Audiences loved the rural bumpkin with a heart of gold from the start. Gomer was the perfect foil for dumb deputy Barney Fife, whom he idolized. It was all a whirlwind for Nabors, who could not get over where he was and what he was doing, since he had no prior acting experience.

"Goll-lee!" as Gomer might exclaim.

Andy in his infinite wisdom knew they had an outright star on their hands. He knew if they did not do something with Jim Nabors soon, somebody else would snatch him right up.

He went to producer Aaron Ruben and told him, "I want you to write something for Jim."

In an interview with the Archive of American Television, Ruben said, "Where do you put a guy like Gomer? I thought that that conflict, the juxtaposition of these two unlike subjects, a guy like Gomer and the Marines would make for some pretty good comedy."

Andy's own work in *No Time for Sergeants* was also an inspiration. Thus, the concept for *Gomer Pyle, U.S.M.C.* was born.

Ruben went on to say, "With Gomer, you have such an innocent, good, almost Christ-like character. Where else could you put him but the Marines?"

If being a member of the Mayberry troupe was surreal, being the star of his own series must have made Jim Nabors feel like he had just flown to outer space.

It took a season or two before they allowed him to incorporate his natural singing voice into the show. Once this happened, he also began making record albums. Best-selling ones at that. Altogether, Jim Nabors recorded more than thirty albums over his career: four went gold and one went platinum.

As one can see ... eventually Jim's love for singing was incorporated into the show.

He loved being Gomer Pyle and embraced the role, but longed for more. At the end of the 1968–1969 season and one hundred and fifty episodes in, he wanted to move on.

It was time to headline his own hour-long variety show on CBS. For two years it proved popular, and he even brought old pals Frank Sutton and Ronnie Schell along for the rollicking ride.

One unfortunate incident that darkened the mood at the height of the show's popularity, was a stupid and unsubstantiated rumor. What started out as a party joke was circulated to a Hollywood movie gossip magazine.

Jim Nabors and Rock Hudson had both recently attended the same party. The charming, masculine, fifties' matinee idol had been a guest on the variety show in 1971.

The rumor went that the two were secretly married. We told you it was stupid! Hudson's team did immediate damage control and not much else was made of it. It is unknown specifically how it actually affected *The Jim Nabors Hour*, but it was canceled in the spring of '71.

This was also the year of "the rural purge" and though this wasn't quite "rural," Jim had a connection because of Gomer Pyle and it was possibly considered one of the pack. Pat Buttram, who played Mr. Haney on *Green Acres* (1965 – 1971) remarked, "They got rid of every show that had a tree in it."

From the short-lived Jim Nabors Show, *talk format (1978).*

Throughout the seventies, Jim Nabors wasn't in the spotlight as much. He never really left our hearts, as reruns of *Gomer Pyle, U.S.M.C.* aired in syndication like clockwork.

He did sporadic guest spots on variety shows such as *The Sonny and Cher Comedy Hour* (1974), *The Love Boat*, and annual appearances on dear friend Carol Burnett's Saturday night show.

In the fall of 1975, Jim starred with Ruth Buzzi in the Sid and Marty Kroft-produced ABC Saturday morning show *The Lost Saucer*. Two fun-loving aliens named Fi and Fo land on Earth and end up taking two Earth children on a thrilling trip through time.

It only lasted for sixteen episodes. It was universally panned by the critics who even bothered to watch it. Still, a few of the episodes stand out above the others, offering life lessons.

"Fat is Beautiful," Episode 12, shows us that appearances are superficial and size really doesn't matter. It's a shame there weren't enough episodes geared like this one, and most just found *The Lost Saucer* a waste of time. There certainly was no waste of talent.

Besides this, fans wanting to check out Nabors' seventies' work should be on the lookout for a rare, dramatic turn in a 1973 episode of *The Rookies*. It was titled "Downhome Boy" and aired on November 19, 1973.

January, 1978 saw a brief TV talk show hit the airwaves called *The Jim Nabors Show*. The syndicated show did fairly well in the ratings, but only aired reruns its final month of a six-month run. In July, it was replaced by yet another version of *Truth or Consequences*. The second half of time filled by the talk show's departure was *Celebrity Cooking* with a segment filmed featuring Bob Crane of *Hogan's Heroes* (1965–1971). Bob Crane was brutally murdered in Arizona in June, 1978. His segment on the cooking program never aired. It was replaced by another one with comedian Lonnie Shorr.

Burt Reynolds was a superstar in the eighties, producing and starring in a string of silly, star-studded films, mostly hits. Burt recalled in an interview, on hearing of Jim's passing, "I am deeply saddened to hear of Jim Nabors' passing—he was a great friend—we did several movies together. He had a big voice and a bigger zest for life. I love him and so did millions of others."

Reynolds himself would die of an unexpected heart attack, less than a year after his friend passed away.

He did indeed recruit Jim, first for the role of Deputy Fred in *The Best Little Whore-*

Jim appeared alongside his friend Burt Reynolds in the film Stoker Ace *(1983).*

house in Texas (1982). Movies *Stroker Ace* (1983) and *Cannonball Run II* (1984) came later.

Burt also helped Jim achieve a lifelong dream of performing on the dinner theater stage in a 1991 production of *The Music Man* at Reynolds own Jupiter, Florida dinner theater.

Jim Nabors received a star on the Hollywood Walk of Fame in 1991. He was flanked by five fabulously beautiful females at the ceremony: Florence Henderson, Ruth Buzzi, Loni Anderson, Phyllis Diller and Carol Burnett.

In 1972, Jim Nabors was called upon to perform a task that would become an annual tradition for thirty-two years.

He was the guest of Vegas casino owner Bill Harrah at the 1972 Indianapolis 500 race in Indianapolis, Indiana. On race morning, Jim was asked to sing before the big event. He assumed he would be asked to sing The National Anthem.

Instead, race officials asked him to sing "Back Home Again in Indiana." He didn't know the lyrics, so he scrawled them on his hand and wowed the audience with his performance.

While he is so well loved and remembered for singing this song each year at the race, his streak was not a successive one. He sang it every race from 1972-1978. Peter Marshall, the host of *Hollywood Squares,* sang it in 1979.

Dr. Richard Smith performed the song in 1980, Phil Harris in 1981, and Louis Sudler in 1982. Nabors was back in 1983 and 1984. In 1985 we had the Voices of Liberty singing, and in 1986, John Davies.

Jim was back for a long spell from 1987 on. He sang at twenty-seven of twenty-eight Indianapolis 500 races. He missed 2007 due to illness, and his 2012 performance was taped and played on a huge screen because he was too ill to travel.

Jim belting out "Back Home Again in Indiana" at the Indianapolis 500.

2014 was announced as Jim Nabors' final trip to Indianapolis to sing "Back Home Again in Indiana," as his health was taking a toll on him.

The good times were coming to a grinding halt by the early nineties. Jim had made a trip to India where he believed he contracted the disease hepatitis B. His liver was seriously damaged to the point where he was put on the liver transplant list with all likelihood he would die waiting.

About this dreadful time in his life he told Matt Lauer, "You can't really hope for a liver because to hope for a liver means someone has to die."

Carol Burnett told her "good luck charm" that he would not die from liver failure on her watch. She phoned a friend who was high up in the UCLA medical center in the transplant division. She literally saved the star's life.

Given a second chance at life, Jim showed his gratitude by continuing to perform the song at the Indy 500 for a number of years.

Dear friends Carol Burnett and Jim Nabors.

After his heyday, Jim Nabors used his business smarts to begin purchasing mass amounts of real estate, some of which he quickly divested, and some, mostly the Hawaiian property, he kept. These purchases included a multimillion-dollar macadamia nut ranch in Maui.

The actor began vacationing in the islands while his hit show was still on the air. He brought his mother to Hawaii, where she made a second home. Jim soon fell in love with the serenity and beauty that was the fiftieth state. In 1967, he sold his home in Bel Air and bought one on Diamond Head.

"I just walked off the plane and knew this was where I wanted to be," He told the *Hawaiian News Now* team in an interview once. "It was the air and the friendship and the friendliness of the people, you know. I just knew there was something inside me that told me 'Hey, you're gonna end up here.'"

He concluded by saying, "I love everything about it."

It was here in 1975 he met a Honolulu firefighter named Stan Cadwallader who would eventually work for him and become his constant companion.

In early 2013, Jim and Stan traveled to Washington state and were married. Nabors called *Hawaiian News Now* and gave them a simple statement.

"I'm eighty-two and he's in his sixties, and so we've been together for thirty-eight years. I'm not ashamed of people knowing. It's just that it was a personal thing. I didn't tell anybody. I'm very happy that I've had a partner for thirty-eight years, and I feel very blessed.

"And just want to tell you that I'm very happy."

Jim's waning years were beset by health problems. Besides the liver failure, he also underwent open-heart surgery in May, 2012.

One of his biggest contributions to the Aloha state was a show he did each Christmas season at the Hawaii Theatre in Honolulu from 1997–2006, called *A Merry Christmas with Friends and Nabors*.

He was as popular with the tourists and locals as native son, Don Ho.

The end came for Jim Nabors, our beloved Gomer Pyle, on Nov. 30, 2017. He was dead at the age of eighty-seven.

Heartfelt condolences poured in from around the world. Elizabeth MacRae who had played Lou Ann Poovie, Gomer's love interest, answered her door that morning to a rather somber postman.

He told her, "I'm so glad you're home. I want to tell you I'm so sad about Gomer."

She was shocked. She later told Bill Kirby of the *Fayetteville Observer*, "I loved working with Jim. We just clicked. Aaron Ruben was our senior producer. I went to read for another part and I was trying not to have a southern accent. But Lee Phillips, another North Carolina actor, looked in and said,

Elizabeth MacRae and Jim "clicked" in the nicest way.

'My Lord, that's my favorite southern belle.' Aaron said, 'Can you speak with a southern accent?'"

Lou Ann was originally a short-term role that turned into a regular part.

During the 1968 season of *Gomer Pyle, U.S.M.C.*, MacRae lost her husband, screenwriter Nedrick Young (*The Defiant Ones*, 1958) to a massive coronary. Shortly after, her baby also died.

Thankfully, for boomers and newbies alike, the Camp Henderson hijinks continue!

Jim and his mother Mavis offered her a space to live and heal in their own home, but she declined. In the interview with Kirby, she reiterated about how kind both Jim and his mother had been to her.

The show sort of went off radar, so to speak, for a number of years after the eighties. When MeTV came along, they began bringing back so many of the classic series baby boomers grew up with.

Gomer Pyle was back, not only for old fans, but a new generation as well.

One more note before we end this chapter: in 2001, Jim Nabors received what was probably the greatest honor he could have been awarded, given his most famous role. The United States Marine Corps made him an honorary lance corporal.

In 2007, he was made an honorary corporal, and in 2013, an honorary sergeant.

Rest in peace, Sergeant Pyle.

(7)
SEASON TWO

The second season of *Gomer Pyle, U.S.M.C.* kicked off its first color broadcast on Wednesday, Sept. 17, 1965. It was directed by Aaron Ruben and written by the crackerjack team of Ben Joelson and Art Baer. "PFC Pyle" finds Carter postponing his vacation until his platoon passes their PFC exams. There is one hold-out: Gomer Pyle.

Frank Sutton with Jack Larson in his only appearance on the series: "PFC Gomer Pyle" (Sept. 17, 1965).

Of special note, this is the only appearance of Jack Larson as a corporal. Larson's most famous television role was as budding newshound Jimmy Olsen on *The Adventures of Superman* (1951 – 1957). He was also a well-received playwright.

The next episode—#32 for those keeping count—marks the first-time screen appearance on the series for veteran character actor Allan Melvin, as Sgt. Charlie Hacker. Hacker runs his mess hall like a taut ship, even if it be a ship filled with leaks.

In "Third Finger, Left Loaf" (Sept. 24, 1965), Gomer misplaces Lombardi's wedding ring, believing it to be lost in one of six hundred loaves of bread he helped bake.

Man of many characters: Allan Melvin, here as Sgt. Charlie Hacker.

Lombardi's first name has now changed from Joey to Frankie, and he's played by Ted Bessell.

He was a year or so away from becoming Ann Marie's boyfriend on *That Girl* (1966–1971).

During Season 2, we can watch for numerous familiar faces to show up as guest stars.

We have Dabbs Greer, Tige Andrews (in a three-story navy arc), George Lindsey as Goober Pyle, Michael, Conrad and Enid Markey. Also on the small screen are Ronnie Howard, Andy Griffith, Susan Oliver, Douglas Fowley, Jamie Farr, and Marilyn Mason.

That fall, in the fortieth episode titled "Gomer the Star Witness" (Nov. 19, 1965), Roy Stuart debuted as Corporal Chuck Boyle.

Barbara Stuart, who had been in two previous episodes as the Dragon Lady and Bunny Harper, becomes Bunny Wilson from this point on, and Carter's long-suffering girlfriend.

Jim Nabors (Gomer) with Roy Stuart (Corporal Boyle).

"Gomer the Star Witness" also features actress Arlene Golonka. She would later play Millie, girlfriend to Sam Jones (Ken Berry) on the spin-off, *Mayberry R.F.D.* (1968–1971).

Most fans have stated over the years how much they liked the episodes set off base. With progression, more and more situations arose away from Camp Henderson.

Season 2 saw a three-story arc take place aboard ship for the crew. The main guest star was Tige Andrews as CPO Wayne "Rattlesnake" Simpson. Andrews would have his hands full a few years later playing boss to hippies turned cops in *The Mod Squad* (1968–1973).

"Cat Overboard" (Oct. 29, 1965) finds animal lover Gomer Pyle at it again, rescuing strays. This time it is an orange tabby cat he

The seldom-amused Colonel Gray (Forrest Compton) with Tige Andrews.

names Henrietta. The chief petty officer is furious, threatening to throw all contraband overboard.

In the end, Henrietta melts all hearts including Nelson's and Carter's.

The other two outings at sea are strong stories, with the last being the strongest.

"Gomer Captures a Submarine" (Nov. 5, 1965) features a goof by Carter when he says that he has been in the U.S.M.C. for fifteen years, which would put it at 1950. Yet he wears WWII decorations in the series.

"The Grudge Match" (Nov. 12, 1965) has Sgt. Carter challenging CPO Nelson to a boxing match. Carter was a welterweight champion in high school, while Nelson was the fleet champion who only stopped fighting because no one would fight him!

It's predictable how this one is going to come out. It has two elements Private Pyle definitely does not approve of: gambling and deception.

"Judy, Judy, Judy!" George Lindsey as Cousin Goober Pyle in "A Visit From Cousin Goober" (Nov. 26, 1965).

In another entertaining plotline, one of the sergeant's biggest challenges comes with a visit from cousin Goober. Carter believes Goober is only a figment of Pyle's imagination. Goober causes a multitude of problems from the moment he arrives and decides to try on Gomer's uniform.

He wears this uniform complete with his fancy brown-and-white shoes.

By the time all the complications are figured out, Carter is quite relieved to discover "There really is a Goober!"

George Lindsey of course comes straight out of Mayberry, and while the first visitor from back home, he would not be the last. Opie runs away from home and wants to join the Marines. Andy has to come to Camp Henderson to take his wayward son back.

In the first episode of Season 4, Aunt Bee visits.

George had only appeared with Jim on *The Andy Griffith Show*, but was mentioned often and is considered his successor at the fillin' station. For the remainder of his career, George Lindsey was more Goober than Jim Nabors was Gomer.

Few roles found him playing anything else. He found steady work in Kornfield Kounty on the long-running *Hee Haw* (1969–1997).

The author of this book will now examine his personal favorite of the Pyle episodes: "Gomer Minds His Sergeant's Car" (Dec. 10, 1965).

When Carter has to fly to San Francisco to pick up a Marine who is AWOL (Absent Without Leave), he assigns Pyle to drive his beloved car back to base. The car is stolen and Pyle has twenty-four hours to find it.

A beautiful, red 1960 Dodge Dart Seneca, the Phoenix appears in three episodes total. Careful observation will show that the cars are switched before the demolition scene. Apparently producers didn't want to destroy such a beautiful automobile.

Another episode that calls to us, "Gomer and the Phone Company" (Feb. 25, 1966), sees Pyle once again trying to do a good deed and getting flak for it.

Carter's once-beautiful 1960 Dodge Seneca after being demolished in "Gomer Minds his Sergeant's Car."

He attempts to return some money that rightfully belongs to the phone company and gets accused of stealing it.

"You treat me nice, I'll treat you nice. You treat me mean and I'll ignore you," Pyle tells interrogators, and it pretty much sums up his philosophy.

"Gomer and the Phone Company" features a guest spot by Parley Baer who was Mayor Stoner on the Griffith Show.

There are other second-season winners which we should note. "Duke Slater, Nightclub Comic" (March 4, 1966) lets Ronnie Schell shine in his comedic glory as he perfects an impressionist act with impersonations of his own sergeant, of all people.

"Move it, move it, move it!"

Ronnie Schell, with help from Milton Frome, gauges audience response to his impressions in "Duke Slater, Nightclub Comic" (March 4, 1966).

"Vacation in Vegas" (March 11, 1966) has Carter trying to outwit Gomer in Las Vegas, but Gomer stays a step ahead of him.

If you go to Vegas, please be sure to include Hoover Dam on your sightseeing list. Carter loved it!

"Gomer and the Father Figure" (April 1, 1966) finds both he and Carter being duped by an alcoholic bum.

The following season, the series would move to Wednesday nights, where it would drop down to number 10 in the ratings. While respectable, this is the lowest rating number for the history of *Gomer Pyle, U.S.M.C.*

Its chief competition was *Peyton Place* (1964–1969) and a network movie. In the fall of 1967, it would move back to Friday for the rest of its run and bounce back to number 3 most popular show in the land for its fourth season, and number 2 for its fifth and final one.

(8)
FRANK SUTTON

The sun shone through the second time around and the weather cooperated in Clarksville, Tennessee, as citizens gathered around to honor a favorite son. Frank Sutton, actor and war hero, was born here on Oct. 23, 1923. His fans met on Franklin Street for the unveiling of a statue of Sutton in the character of his most famous personage, Sgt. Vince Carter.

Mark Holleman of Coldwell Banker Conroy, Marable and Holleman drove the effort after speaking with Pat Powers, a distant relative of Sutton's.

Holleman recalled, "We decided to do it, conferred with the city about how to make it happen, then formed a committee, found some investors, and raised some money."

Frank Spencer Sutton was born an only child to parents Frank and Thelma, who met while working at the local newspaper.

After moving to Nashville, the acting bug bit young Frank. He first stepped onstage at the tender age of eight. Once enrolled at East Nashville High, he became an active member of the drama club.

"The first time I walked onstage, I had a warm feeling. I knew that I wanted to be an actor."

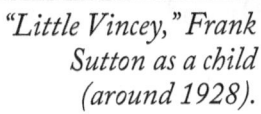

"Little Vincey," Frank Sutton as a child (around 1928).

Sutton's father died not long after moving to Nashville, and his death hit his son especially hard. Frank vowed to be the best father he could possibly be to his own kids, which he was.

When he graduated high school in 1941, he returned to Clarksville and went to work as a radio announcer. Ironically, the man who would charm millions playing a tough Marine drill instructor tried enlisting, and was rejected due to a medical reason. He

Truly a commanding presence, whether as a real-life, or TV sergeant.

Early publicity shot of Frank Sutton.

then tried the army, where he served with distinction in the South Pacific during World War II.

Frank Sutton participated in fourteen assault landings. He received the rank of sergeant and was later awarded the Bronze Star and Purple Heart.

Once discharged and firmly ensconced back into civilian life, he resumed his acting career in earnest. To further his chances, he studied at prestigious Columbia University, earning a Bachelor's Degree in 1952.

One of his first notable roles was on the early kids' television show, *Tom Corbett, Space Cadet* (1950-1955). He played Cadet Eric Raddison. He also did some other episodic work in fifties' TV. These actors were called "day players," and most earned around twenty-five dollars per hour.

Future work ensued in two soaps: *The Edge of Night* (1956–1984) and *The Secret Storm* (1954–1974). One of the soap writers he worked with was Toby Igler, whom he had met at Columbia and married.

Classic movie lovers remember Frank's performance as Ralph, friend to the character Marty in the movie version of *Marty* (1955). Speculate if you will, but it is fairly obvious Sutton could easily have played the lead role instead of Ernest Borgnine, who won the Oscar as the lonely butcher who finds love at last.

A few key roles to watch for would be Frank's appearances in *Gunsmoke* (1955–1975) as the lead guest star in "Old Comrade" (Dec. 29, 1962). He was also in "Catawomper" (Feb. 10, 1962) and "Miss Kitty" (Oct. 14, 1961).

1962 saw him in four episodes of *The Untouchables* (1959–1963). He is also quite good as a deputy in a 1963 episode of *The Fugitive* (1963–1967) titled "The Other Side of the Mountain" (Oct. 1, 1963).

Aficionados of *The Twilight Zone* (1959-1964) recall Frank's role as the manager in the chilling episode titled "The Dummy" (May 4, 1962), co-starring with Cliff Robertson. In this, which inspired the movie *Magic* (1979), a ventriloquist dummy has a mind of his own.

After fifteen-plus years of second-fiddle roles, everything came together for Frank Sutton when Sgt. Carter came along. He portrayed the perfect combination of exasperation and pathos. In the hands of a lesser actor, Sgt. Carter could have been an unlikable cuss. He dominated every scene he was in with subtleties and nuances that clinched his fame. Gomer could not help but like him, and neither could we.

He and Nabors became such close friends, that when five years had quickly flown by and Nabors wanted to move on to a variety show, he asked both Frank Sutton and Ronnie Schell to be regulars. It was kismet.

Frank Sutton and Jim Nabors became buddies in real life.

For two seasons, *The Jim Nabors Hour* (1969–1971) was watched by adoring fans. It wasn't the same as Gomer, but with these greats at the helm, it was very close.

After television roles waned, in part to typecasting as Carter, Sutton went back to his first love—the stage. He traveled the dinner theater circuit, and when he was home, shared a beautiful mansion in Beverly Hills with his wife Toby, daughter Amanda, and son Joe.

A little-known fact about Frank Sutton's life was his devotion to the military. At the height of the Vietnam War, he tried to put a show together for the USO to go overseas and entertain the troops. When there was no funding readily available, he funded the trip himself and went.

The Marines were on hand to help by providing a helicopter to fly Sutton to battle zones. Columnist Vernon Scott wrote of this trip in 1966, "'I still get qualms about going into a combat zone,' said Sutton on the eve of his departure. 'And the same sleepy feeling comes over me that I used to get on landing boats when we were taking an island.'"

Sutton's Vietnam show consisted of songs, patter, poetry, a monologue, and comedy as his familiar Sergeant Carter character.

Sutton told Scott he was doing this because when he was on the beaches in World War II, he remembered comic Joe E. Brown appearing like a beacon to entertain. The *Gomer Pyle* actor had also performed at home for wounded vets in military hospitals. His patriotism really showed through, as he knew the importance of morale and wanted to give to a greater cause.

Vince gets in on the act. Left to right: Milton Frome, Frank Sutton, Jim Nabors, and Ronnie Schell in "Duke Slater, Nightclub Comic" (March 4, 1966).

Scott called Frank Sutton nothing like "the mallet-headed Carter", saying he was "bright and articulate and happy about the warm reception he had received from servicemen."

For his take on the irascible Vincent Carter, Sutton told Scott, "Maybe a Marine sergeant can get away with treating his troops as rough as he does. But I was in the Signal Corps, and if a sergeant tried to throw his weight around like that, he'd have been punched in the mouth."

As mentioned, the decade of the seventies was not as easy for Frank Sutton. He continued to work wherever he could, and did several guest spots on game shows such as *Password*. He can be found in three stories on the popular *Love, American Style* (1969–1971).

These were "Love and the Haunted House" (Nov. 6, 1970), "Love and the Lady Barber" (Nov. 19, 1971), and "Love and the Guru" (Jan. 26, 1972).

Of the three, the "Haunted House" episode is the strongest, with excellent support from Ruth Buzzi and none other than Vincent Price himself!

The "Lady Barber" episode pairs Frank with Joe Besser who was one of the Three Stooges, and the Guru episode has a part for James Hampton, who was bugler Dobbs on *F Troop* and guest-starred on Pyle.

Internet blogs continue to draw in fans' comments about *Gomer Pyle, U.S.M.C.* and especially Frank Sutton. Many know he died young and not long after the show, but are sketchy on his career as a whole.

This remembrance was posted by "Unknown" on a blog maintained by Scott Rollins.

"I can't heeeear you!"

"Frank Sutton was a wonderful actor. As Sgt. Carter, he brought laughter to my life as a child in *Gomer Pyle*. Even to this day when I catch an episode, he still makes me laugh and feel so good, especially after a hard and difficult day. Right from childhood, I wondered over the years if all that yelling he did as Sgt. Carter caused harm to his health.

"As an adult, I wondered if the yelling caused his blood pressure to rise and ultimately damaged his heart. He was too young to die. I just think of all the laughter the world has missed out on because of his untimely death. Anyway, I hope he is happy and still making people laugh in heaven."

Much has been written about the dangers of method acting. It is a technique developed in part by Lee Strasberg, based on the teachings of a master known as Stanislavski. Actors fully immerse themselves into the character they are playing.

Marlon Brando may be the most famous method actor. For his first film *The Men* (1950), in which he played a paraplegic, he spent a month in a hospital with military patients learning how they relied on upper body strength to manage their bodies.

Jamie Foxx glued his eyes shut for fourteen hours straight in his preparation to play singer Ray Charles in the movie *Ray* (1996). He also lost thirty pounds and had a cosmetic dentist purposely chip his teeth to make him look more like Charles.

Daniel Day-Lewis is perhaps the most famous modern method actor. He has always delved so deeply into his characters that he recently announced his retirement because all of this acting has taken a toll on him.

Sarge rages on!

So it is safe to assume that Frank Sutton, who came from the era when method acting was being taught ferociously—the successful ones becoming superstars on film—would have practiced what was preached.

In researching this book, the author has consulted psychologists' reports, and no correlation has been found to prove that all the yelling and feigned anger Frank really got into as Sgt. Carter, later caused his fatal heart attack.

It is more reasonable to believe that it was because of his Type A personality, being a high-strung person who drank enormous amounts of coffee and loved smoking cigars.

It was in Shreveport, Louisiana on June 28, 1974, at the Beverly Barn Dinner Playhouse while preparing for a performance of the play *Luv,* that Sutton died unexpectedly of a heart attack. He was fifty years old.

His family had journeyed to Louisiana to be with him. He was buried in Greenwood Cemetery in his hometown of Clarksville, Tennessee.

Frank Sutton's early death left a void in the entertainment world. No longer would we hear him bark out orders or see those veins stick out in his neck. Except of course, in perpetual reruns.

No more roles were to come in for him to perfect his acting chops further. His last role was the television movie *Hurricane* (1974) which aired on ABC posthumously.

Sutton plays party animal Bert Pearson, who ignores all warnings from the National Weather Service, his friends and family, and from reading the script. He plans a huge hurricane party instead of evacuating his Mississippi home.

Here, Vince plays it cool.

He shares the screen with Martin Milner, Larry Hagman, Jessica Walter, Barry Sullivan, Will Geer, and Michael Learned.

Disaster films were all the rage at the time, but this one was not well received. More than a third of the film consists of stock footage which looks shoddily filmed by TV news crews.

What we have here is bickering and fretting and worrying and more worrying, countered by Pearson's "so what?" attitude.

If there is a saving grace one can attach to *Hurricane*, it would be Frank Sutton's performance. The character is totally unlikable and gets his comeuppance.

One more TV film was released with Frank Sutton in it in 1974. It was a comedy called *Ernie, Madge and Artie* (1974) and co-starred Cloris Leachman and Dick Van Patton. The plot revolved around the ghost of a woman's dead husband threatening her new marriage.

Frank Sutton, best known for playing Sergeant Carter on *Gomer Pyle, U.S.M.C.*, had a brilliant career worth close examination. Two more roles worthy of note would be his heavy portrayal as one of the rapists in the Kirk Douglas film *Town Without Pity* (1958), and the espionage thriller *The Satan Bug* (1965).

We would have loved to have had Frank Sutton, best known as Sergeant Carter, around longer. Even the men in his platoon felt the same way didn't they?

Well almost.

We close with some words from "Sergeant Carter's Farewell to his Troops" (Jan. 15, 1965). Carter has had it with being a Marine (for fourteen years this time; it keeps changing) and he is ready to go to Anaheim to be a motorcycle cop. Motorcycle cops get all the girls.

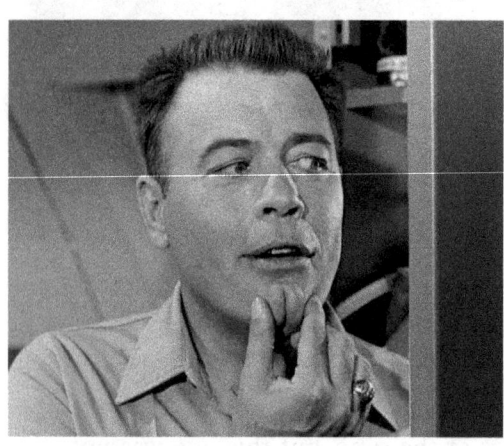

Carter (Frank Sutton) admires his Kirk Douglas-like chin.

Of course, Gomer doesn't want to see him go. He tries to convince the others to make Carter stay for another hitch.

In the end, we know Carter is going to be around a while longer—at least for the remainder of the series. Newly reenlisted, he tells his men as he's bawling them out, "You know what it's going to be like around here? Well, I'll tell you. Picture everything that's gone on before as a little pink tea party with ladyfingers. Because from now on you're going to shape up! And I'm going to be on all your backs."

Gomer grins and says, "Sure seems like old times."

Yes Gomer, it sure does.

(9)
SEASON THREE

Only Gomer Pyle could step off a bus, meet a movie star, and get invited to her home for the day. He is so excited and can't wait to spread the news—except no one believes him.

Deborah Walley, fresh from the beach as in *Beach Blanket Bingo* (1965), shines as perky Tina Tracy in "Lies, Lies, Lies" (Sept. 14, 1965).

Tina Tracy is Gomer's favorite movie star. Huh? She beat out Godzilla?

Once the misunderstanding is cleared up and Carter and gang find out Gomer was telling the truth as always, Tina throws a lovely party for the Marines.

One final note on this episode: Sgt. Carter really needs to watch his step around swimming pools.

During Season 3, our midway point, Gomer gets to race in the inter-squad competition, battles the German measles, meets Friendly Freddy, is accused of turning a man into an alcoholic, sees little green men, gets arrested, becomes engaged, learns to cook, gets kidnapped along with Carter by smugglers, and predicts the

Misunderstandings are cleared up poolside with movie star Tina Tracy (Deborah Walley) in "Lies, Lies, Lies" (Sept. 14, 1966).

Friendly Freddy always had an angle and cheap deals. Sid Melton with Jim Nabors in "Caution: Low Overhead" (Oct. 5, 1966).

weather beautifully. One thing he did remain blissfully ignorant about: the art of plugging a melon!

With all these shenanigans occurring, it is no understatement to say Season 3 is one of the best.

"Show Me the Way to Go Home" (Oct. 12, 1966) has the ever-helpful Gomer trying to see that an inebriated Keenan Wynn gets home safe and sound.

What does he get for his trouble? Pounced on by the man's wife, Iona, who according to Harry is "the sweetest little woman in the whole world."

Could this exercise in futility not just be a life lesson for the hapless private to leave things well enough alone, as Slater tells him? Not on your life!

See, Harry Purcell shows up at the base to apologize. "Hey Gomer, I'm really sorry about what happened last night. You know what happened? I drank on an empty stomach. Goes right to my head. Happens every time. Let me make it up to you by buying you a steak dinner tonight."

Pert Kelton is a hoot as the irate wife. She goes to see Carter, who is disbelieving of her story despite her insistence that "Harry doesn't drink!"

Boyle tries to convince ol' Vince that maybe Pyle has taken to the sauce.

"Not in a million years," Carter tells him.

Then he sees Pyle dancing with Purcell in a diner.

When he approaches them, Gomer chastises, "You thought I was drinking—shame, shame, shame!"

"Harry doesn't drink!" Gomer befriends a drunk with disastrous results in "Show Me the Way to Go Home" (Oct. 12, 1966), with standout performance by Keenan Wynn as Harry Purcell.

While a totally funny episode, "Show Me the Way to Go Home" reveals an ugly truth about alcoholism. Many alcoholics are just like

Harry Purcell. They are functional. Sober and straight by daylight and plastered by night.

It is good we can laugh at our foibles, yet still realize the world is not always sunshine and roses. If everyone operated the way Gomer Pyle does, then it might actually reach that state.

One week later came a prize of an episode, titled "How to Succeed in Farming Without Really Trying" (Oct. 19, 1966).

This is an episode that ranks high with fans and has been constantly talked about since it first aired. Now admit it, how many of you after seeing it, ever tried plugging a melon?

The sergeant wishes to quash Gomer's budding love of gardening by resorting to the age-old trick (at least an age-old Carter trick) of plugging a watermelon with vodka. That would be cutting a small portion out, pouring vodka in, and replacing the plug. The idea is to make Gomer sick—sick enough to give up gardening.

Carter and Boyle, (Sutton and Stuart) plugging a melon in "How to Succeed in Farming Without Really Trying" (Oct. 19, 1966).

Not a chance.

Gomer stares in disbelief at how the enormous melon has grown virtually overnight.

"You know, Pyle," Carter theorizes, "I bet that super-nitrate stuff you used all went to one spot and this melon got it all."

Even Pyle knows this reasoning is full of holes as he goes to great lengths to give the "plugged" watermelon to his sergeant.

After narrowly avoiding falling into his own trap, Carter must chase down the bad melon all over the base before the wrong person bites into it.

There is a funny scene set in Hacker's mess hall, the result being a lot of watermelons ruined and Hacker chasing both Gomer and Carter out of the hall with a meat cleaver.

Chaos ensues when the melon winds up going to a party at Colonel Gray's, given by his wife. Carter has to retrieve the melon, and fast!

One last, feeble attempt by Carter to switch melons fails miserably. Later in Colonel Gray's office, he tells Gomer and Carter, "It's the first time in seven years one of my wife's bridge luncheons ended with singing. When Major Brady came to pick up his wife, he said she danced to the car."

Colonel Gray (Forrest Compton) muses about the unusual effect on the ladies' bridge luncheon after they sampled that melon!

This ranks up there in sitcom history with the *Barney Miller* (1975–1982) episode "Hash" (Dec. 30, 1976), and is reminiscent of the scene from the movie *Spencer's Mountain* (1963) in which Henry Fonda accidentally gets the new preacher (Wally Cox) drunk.

It would have been a hoot and much funnier had the intoxicated ladies actually be shown. Still, so many fans of *Gomer Pyle, U.S.M.C.* remember and cherish "How to Succeed in Farming Without Really Trying." The title is a takeoff on a successful Broadway musical and later movie titled "How to Succeed in Business Without Really Trying" (1967). The movie starred Robert Morse and Rudy Vallee.

"I bet this one is definitely Clarice!" Sutton and Stuart in "The Secret Life of Gomer Pyle" (Jan. 11, 1967).

"The Secret Life of Gomer Pyle" (Jan. 11, 1967) has Carter and Boyle wondering what Pyle really does on his free Sundays. In other words, are "Sundays fundays"?

A misunderstanding over pictures in a girlie magazine has them thinking Gomer is spending his time with a bevy of bikinied babes.

Imagine their total shock when they discover Gomer has really been spending his time hooking rugs with a bunch of elderly women.

Roy Stuart has some great moments as he is mesmerized by which one might be Clarice.

The real Clarice is played by none other than Mayberry's own Hope Summers, who played nosy Clara Edwards.

The character of Lou Ann Poovie makes her first appearance during this season.

"Love's Old Sweet Song" (Dec. 22, 1966) portrays her as a torch singer, albeit not a very good one. The part of Lou Ann, it seems, was slated to be a one-time role, or at least recurring. At the end of this episode, she returns to North Carolina to marry her ex-boyfriend. However, she proved popular and returned eight episodes later in "Lou Ann Sings Again" (Feb. 22, 1967).

While she is attracting her fair share of admirers, it soon becomes apparent both Carter and Slater are going to lose, as she only has eyes for Gomer.

By the last episode of Season 3, "Lou Ann Sings No More" (April 12, 1967), she is fired from her lounge-singing job. Carter and Slater try to convince her she should pursue a record deal. It is finally Gomer who proves to her she cannot sing and gets her a job in a record store.

And a steady girl in the process.

Elizabeth MacRae belts one out in "Lou Ann Poovie Sings Again" (Feb. 22, 1967).

One of the most significant episodes of the season that must be considered is "Gomer, the Welsh Rarebit Fiend" (March 1, 1967).

There is an old wives' tale that eating Welsh rarebit past a certain time of night can lead to bad nightmares. Both Gomer and

Sgt. Carter partake of the dish (mostly toast lavishly topped with cheese), and it affects them differently.

While sleepwalking, they change personalities. Gomer bawls Vince out about the way he berates him constantly. Carter is only meek and apologetic, promising to do better.

Is there any fact to this legend? Probably none in the least. This writer and a friend decided to try this deliciously rich dish, consuming it late one evening. Waiting for bad dreams that never came, it's safe to assume we didn't sleepwalk and tell anyone off... that we know of!

"And another thing, Carter... I'm tired of the way you're always yellin' at me. You hear? What's that? I can't hear you!" From "Gomer, the Welsh Rarebit Fiend" (March 1, 1967).

The series was hitting a number of highlights under the writing mastery of Mittleman, Idelson, and Ruben. The following week, "Sing a Song of Papa" (March 8, 1967) was aired.

Gomer wins an amateur contest singing the song "Oh My Papa" in a nightclub. The club owner, who is characterized as a mobster (Anthony Caruso), is so emotionally overcome that he wants the private to sing it in his club every night.

When Carter balks, a game of intimidation begins. The song reminds Nino of his dear old Papa back in Italy. The problem is solved when Gomer manages to find a way to reunite the two.

Anthony Caruso as Nino, and Ronnie Schell as Duke, in "Sing a Song of Papa" (March 8, 1967).

"Oh Mein Papa" was a German song written in 1939,

and is originally sung by a woman looking back on memories of her clown father. Eddie Fisher had a Number One Billboard Hit in 1954 with the name change.

"Sing A Song of Papa" is a highly emotional episode, one of the heartwarming type we have grown to expect from such an exceptional series.

Gomer Pyle was always the safe choice when it came to escorting officers' daughters. In "Lost, the Colonel's Daughter" (March 22, 1967), he is asked to take out Colonel Gray's daughter Janice (Suzanne Benoit).

Janice has been attending an all-women's college and is progressive in true sixties' fashion. She cons Gomer into taking her to a discotheque, where she promptly loses him. He calls Carter to help him locate her, and they do—at an even wilder party with hippies.

One thing leads to another, and they wind up getting arrested for disturbing the peace.

Rob Reiner, a few years away from his groundbreaking role as Mike Stivic on *All in the Family*, is seen as a hippie who has an intense and interesting conversation with Gomer.

Gomer (Jim Nabors) and Janice (Suzanne Benoit) visit a go-go club in "Lost, the Colonel's Daughter" (March 22, 1967).

As Season 3 wrapped up, 1967 was on the cusp of the Summer of Love. Times were changing, but a close look at the Nielsen Ratings would not have reflected this.

The Number One show for the 1966–1967 television season was *Bonanza* (1959–1972), and Number Ten was *The Lawrence Welk Show* (1955–1975). Gomer tied for Number Nine with *The Virginian* (1962–1971).

The fourth season to begin in September would see the return of familiar faces and even more familiar plots. The writing, direction and acting would remain above par.

Camp Henderson was holding firm.

(10)
RONNIE SCHELL

Ronnie Schell has been dubbed "the slowest rising comedian in show business." He's earned that moniker through sheer consistency and true dedication to his work, a career dating back to the fifties' club scene.

"I never turn down work," Schell has said.

Of course, Gomer Pyle fans recognize him immediately as private-turned-corporal Gilbert "Duke" Slater. He was among the third tier of stars holding his own beside Jim Nabors and Frank Sutton. His role was an important one.

Duke played mediator, as those two were always at odds. He kept the peace. He would also make the occasional wisecrack along the way.

Meeting Ronnie Schell and spending a warm, June evening reminiscing with him about Hollywood's golden days and *Gomer Pyle, U.S.M.C.* was a sheer joy for this writer. Conversation came easily, and he took us on a journey backward in time to when he was a struggling young comic.

Duke Slater, shown here as corporal, plants his peacemaking self between Sarge and Gomer.

He was working the club circuit in California when fellow comic Phyllis Diller was appearing on Groucho Marx's quiz show *You Bet Your Life* (1950–1961).

She suggested Ronnie try to get on the show and spar with Groucho, which he ultimately did. He won six hundred dollars and guessed the secret word. His area of expertise was Beatnik Jive.

"Groucho couldn't have been more gracious. He was a real nice guy," Schell remembered.

By 1964, when *Gomer Pyle, U.S.M.C.* was new to the airwaves, so was thirty-two-year-old Ronnie Schell. He was one of the recruits from boot camp on. The first few episodes, he wasn't given much to do as the plots needed to revolve around Jim and Frank. Slowly, the character of Duke was allowed to evolve and given texture.

Given Schell's comic nature, Slater was a wisecracker. In the hands of a lesser comedian, Duke could have come and gone quickly. Ronnie was a natural impressionist and this was written into "Duke Slater, Night Club Comic" (March 4, 1966). One of his best impressions is of Sergeant Carter. So it's a bad idea when Gomer invites Carter to the Jade Club to check out the act.

Producers of the show quickly capitalized on Ronnie Schell's comedic talent, having Duke Slater's character revel in being the barracks cutup.

Milton Frome, a veteran character actor seen in too many series to mention, plays a club emcee.

How could a show that was created by Bill Persky, Sam Denoff, Carl Reiner, and Sheldon Leonard flop? And how could the same show with writers such as Bill Idelson, James L. Brooks, Carl Kleinschmidt, Rick Mittleman, Peggy Elliott, and Dale McRaven flop?

Well, one did.

Whether playing Duke Slater or himself, Ronnie Schell, here at the Jade Club with Milton Frome, never fails to move the needle on audience response!

These were the best sitcom writers and producers of the sixties. When Ronnie Schell was offered the lead role in the sitcom *Good Morning World* (1967–1968), he jumped at it.

"I told Jim, whom I was by now a really close friend of, that I was reluctantly leaving Gomer Pyle, because now I was going to be the star," Schell recalled.

Good Morning World was a one-season wonder. It had a lot going for it, but failed to catch on and disappeared into television obscurity, until Antenna TV revived it and started airing repeats in January, 2017.

Schell played radio DJ Larry Clarke. Together with Joby Baker as DJ David Lewis, they hosted a morning drive-time radio show called *Lewis and Clarke* on a small AM station in L.A.

The show's creators had all worked as writers at WNEW in New York in earlier days, and many scripts were based on real-life experiences.

There was a young blonde actress who played Ronnie's girlfriend. Her name was Goldie Hawn.

"She didn't like to rehearse," he said. "I told her, 'Goldie I know this business, and if you don't rehearse, you're not going to make it.' A year later she won the Academy Award for *Cactus Flower*."

Various reasons have been attributed to why *Good Morning World* did not make it. Schell claims there was a very good likelihood that the show was going to be picked up for a second season, but it may have meant a massive overhaul.

Joby Baker, Canadian actor, was having trouble memorizing his lines. He had always been a solid side character in everything from Westerns and Walt Disney pictures, to *Girl Happy* (1965) with Elvis Presley, and all three *Gidget* movies.

He left acting in the early eighties and became an abstract painter, having distributed his artwork all over the Los Angeles area.

Julie Parrish (Kentucky born) who played Linda Lewis, Dave's wife, was having health problems. Add this to that novice actress (what was her name again?) whom Ronnie was trying to get to rehearse, and there wasn't much chance for the show.

The almighty Nielsen ratings also foretold the tale: *Good Morning World* had to go. It was replaced by *The Doris Day Show* (1968–1973).

Where else should Ronnie Schell return, but to the popular role of Duke Slater? The Pyle crew was glad to have him back on base. The plot of his return show did not depict him as having such a warm welcome.

"Corporal Duke" (Oct. 4, 1968) was the second episode of the fifth season. When his old reputation gets in the way of the men taking his new position of corporal seriously, Duke takes a hard-line approach. This further alienates him from his old buddies until Gomer steps in and saves the day.

The formerly irreverent Pvt. Duke Slater turns proud corporal.

From here on, things progress nicely, with Duke easing into his mediator role he is most known for. The following episode "The Booty Prize" (Oct. 11, 1968) is a winner, which will be discussed at length in the Season 5 chapter.

By the end of the season, which sadly is the end of the series, it is Duke who reminds Sgt. Carter that even though Gomer Pyle is a foul-up, he usually fixes everything he messes up—maybe not through his own devices—but it all turns out for the best.

Sergeant Carter seems to be kicking some corporal "booty," as hapless Duke helps the cause.

When Nabors chose to leave Pyle behind, it didn't mean leaving Schell behind. He joined him on *The Jim Nabors Hour* (1969–1971)

A dapper Ronnie adds his comic spark to The Carol Burnett Show. *Here, he has the fond and enthusiastic attentions of Carol, and Vicki Lawrence, respectively.*

for comedy skits. He was best known for playing drunken boarder Audie in "The Brothers-In-Law" sketch.

Sold-out shows in Vegas followed as the two toured together in the seventies. He worked as well in episodes of the ABC comedy ensemble *Love, American Style*. He has been in series with Dick Van Dyke, Brian Keith, Larry Hagman, Donna Mills, Paul Lynde, Sally Field, Dom DeLuise, Karen Valentine, Redd Foxx, Robin Williams, Ted Knight, Suzanne Somers, and many, many more.

Ronnie Schell is a walking résumé for having worked with all of the greats in Hollywood for sixty years. It was also in the early seventies that he began a long career as a voice-over artist in cartoons.

He's been heard in *Scooby-Doo, Casper the Friendly Ghost, Wait Till Your Father Gets Home, Shirt Tales, Snorks, Duck Tales,* and *The Smurfs*.

He was a crooked record producer in the second episode of *The Dukes of Hazzard* (1979–1985). The episode was titled "Daisy's Song" (Feb. 2, 1979). His character was called Lester Starr.

In 1984, Ronnie Schell was in the first sitcom produced for WTBS Atlanta, *Down to Earth* (1984–1987). The star was Dick Sargent who had been the second Darrin Stephens on *Bewitched*.

The premise of *Down to Earth* was another supernatural one. An angel who had been a flapper in real life (Carol Mansell) comes to Earth to earn her wings by helping the typical American family, the Prestons.

Ronnie appeared in seventeen episodes.

He was in a number of Disney movies. A couple of these were *Gus* (1976) with Don Knotts, and *The Cat from Outer Space* (1978) with Ken Berry and Sandy Duncan.

From classic TV to cable, movies, cartoons—and even a web series—Ronnie Schell, as of this writing, continues to be the Energizer Bunny of show business.

In 2018, he was one of several familiar faces in the cast of *Kaplan's Korner* (2018 –). The plot revolves around some struggling actors who inherit a talent agency from their late friend, actor Marvin Kaplan.

Joining Ronnie were Robert Pine, Marcia Rodd, Dawn Wells, Lee Meriwether, Sara Ballantine, and Jeanine Anderson.

The dynamic energy bundle that is Ronnie Schell, at times makes it appear he'll go airborne!

Kaplan's Korner was produced as an internet-only series.

Schell also maintains a very active schedule traveling across the U.S. on the nostalgia circuit and Mayberry-related events. He was only in two episodes of *The Andy Griffith Show*, but fans never forget a face.

After Jim Nabors death in late 2017, he has started doing a *Tribute to Jim Nabors* in which he reminisces on stage about *Gomer Pyle, U.S.M.C.* and its stars, and shows film clips.

He also still does a little stand-up. One of the funniest bits is his lip-synching to Caruso while guzzling champagne.

The fun and chemistry of the Gomer Pyle *cast all comes back when Ronnie Schell reminisces in his* Tribute to Jim Nabors.

In an era when elements like class and grace are sorely needed, the world needs more people like Ronnie Schell. He has entertained so many over the years. To think his one-time goal in life was to be a professional baseball player.

"I was a great hitter, but I was slow," Schell says of his Major League attempts. Thus he joined the air force, where doing comedy routines got him out of kitchen duty.

Ronnie attended college at San Francisco State University and graduated Class of '58. In the nineties, he began doing benefits for the school, especially to benefit McKenna Theater where years before he acted in plays and a troupe performing *Kampus Kapers*.

He is very loyal and helpful to those who came up the hard way as he did. In a 2005 interview, he said, "It's very lonely at the middle," then added, "but I'm very fortunate to have never been out of work."

In 1993, television actor Dick Yarmy, who was Don Adams' brother, was dying of lung cancer. Nineteen of his closest comic friends, including Ronnie Schell, took turns around the clock in his hospital room entertaining him and the nurses who cared for him.

They became known as "Yarmy's Army." They continued to meet after their friend's death on a monthly basis for dinners and improvisational comedy.

Any of the standard-bearers from yesterday are invited to join in, and the ranks have included Don Knotts, Phyllis Diller, Jonathan Winters, Shecky Greene, Kaye Ballard, Julius La Rosa, Harvey Korman, Tim Conway, George Segal, and the Unknown Comic.

1998 saw Ronnie calling in the troops for a big benefit for the University. "I feel like I've never given back to the school what I got out of it," he told Sam Whiting of the *SFGATE* Entertainment section.

He also did it as a tribute to former teacher Fenton McKenna, whom the theater is named after. Yarmy's Army keep up the entertaining for, as Ronnie says, "Charity and change."

In addition, Ronnie still does an annual week in Tahoe with his special show. Is there any stopping the unsinkable Ronnie Schell, the unofficial mayor of Encino, California? It is doubtful. He will continue to perform until the day he is no more.

(11)
SEASON FOUR

The fourth season opened with a visit from Aunt Bee, played by the perpetually fluttering Frances Bavier. *Gomer Pyle, U.S.M.C.* was a bona fide hit by this time. Bringing in guests from Mayberry was not done in desperation nor as a cheap ratings boost. With the same producer at the helm, it was smart business.

Seeing the hometown folks in different settings was fun and an homage to how it all started. It would have been nice for Gomer if one of these visits had been better planned and not resulted in so many problems for Sgt. Carter.

"A Visit from Aunt Bee" opened the fourth season (Sept. 8, 1967).

He and Bee clash immediately. "I pictured him much taller," she sighs, referring to how Gomer must have glorified his sergeant in letters back home.

She insists on cleaning the barracks and chastises Carter for his treatment of her friend Gomer. To pour a little more salt in the wound, she grants an interview about same to a TV reporter.

Frances Bavier had a long résumé. Her training had been on the stage. She played a key role in the science fiction classic *The Day the Earth Stood Still* (1951) as well as lots of 1950s television shows.

A guest role on *The Danny Thomas Show* led to her being cast as Aunt Bee. It is the role for which she is best remembered and perhaps the one she loathed the most. Bavier was a difficult party on the set and everyone approached her with caution. After *Mayberry RFD* bit the dust, she retired to North Carolina and became a recluse. She did make an appearance in the family film *Benji* (1974).

She said of the state she made home, "I fell in love with North Carolina, all the pretty roads and the trees."

Rumors have circulated about the complicated relationship between Bavier and Griffith. What the presumed feud for real?

Well, Griffith told the *National Enquirer* once that many years after the series, upon hearing she was in ill health, he took it upon himself to go to her home without calling ahead and knock on her door to ask her why she never liked him.

For his trouble she slammed the door in his face.

Then on *Larry King Live,* he told Larry that four months before she died she called him up and apologized.

Aunt Bee was a tough one.

Sergeant Carter had an ego as big as all outdoors. Mind you, this statement means the character, not the actor. Frank Sutton was a hardworking family man of matinee idol looks in his younger days, who opted to become a comic.

He was no ham, but he could play one. There were many episodes of *Gomer Pyle, U.S.M.C.* in which he was able to display full-blown hamminess. One chance came in the fourth-season showcase "The Recruiting Poster."

Carter definitely thinks he should be the face of Camp Henderson. Imagine his chagrin when Gomer is instead considered!

This one harks back to *The Phil Silvers Show* and an episode titled "The Face on the

Sgt. Carter has a face that belongs on a recruiting poster—according to him. "The Recruiting Poster" (Sept. 15, 1967).

"Who else has a chin like that? Oh yeah, Kirk Douglas!" Boyle watches Carter admire himself.

Recruiting Poster" (Oct. 2, 1956). Hilarity abounds amid the misunderstanding over Doberman's face being selected for a poster.

Of course, it's a mistake because Doberman really does have a face like a Doberman. The toughest general in the military is called in to break the news to him, but it turns out he is an exact lookalike.

This is kind of the same way Vincent Carter was often mistaken for actor Kirk Douglas. It was the chin that made the resemblance.

On Jim Nabors' passing, comedienne Carol Burnett said, "Jim and I remained friends fifty-two years. He was the godfather of my daughter Jody. Every year, he was always the first guest on my variety show. I consider him my 'good luck charm.' My heart is heavy. I'm grateful he was a large part of my life. I miss him. I love him."

Two best friends—Carol Burnett and Jim Nabors.

Carol first appeared on *Gomer Pyle, U.S.M.C.* in "Corporal Carol" (Sept. 22, 1967) as Corporal Carol Barnes. The humor derives from Carol's crush on gullible Private Pyle, and it causes problems between him and steady gal Lou Ann Poovie.

There's a noticeable goof in "Corporal Carol" when Gomer and Carol go to a drive-in movie. They're engrossed in a *Road Runner* cartoon (at least Gomer is), and Gomer tells her that it's is his favorite cartoon because he enjoys how Road Runner is being chased by a fox who can never catch him.

Gomer, that's no fox—it's Wile E. Coyote.

In fall, 1967, *The Carol Burnett Show* first aired, and yes, Jim Nabors was her premiere guest. They played two misfit skiers in a skit called "The Ski Lodge," and Jim sang, "You Don't Have to Say You Love Me" in Italian.

Carol Burnett had been in show business for a while, having worked with Garry Moore, and featured in a highly touted episode of *The Twilight Zone*. She also originated the role of Princess

Winnifred in the musical *Once Upon a Mattress* in her Broadway debut in 1959.

She was nominated for a Tony award for Best Leading Actress in a musical. There was a later TV adaptation in 1963, and a second TV adaptation in 1972 which co-starred Ken Berry.

Carol Burnett would make another *Gomer Pyle, U.S.M.C.* appearance in 1969.

Sutton and Burnett, two pros at play in "Corporal Carol" (Sept. 22, 1967).

The four-story Washington, D.C. arc took the company away from familiar Camp Henderson stomping grounds. One of those episodes dealt with Pyle and Carter being fooled by a young boy and led on a wild goose chase. There is a talent contest that sets up the reason for the trip, and the strongest outing turns out to be "The Show Must Go On" (Nov. 3, 1967).

Before he can display his magnificent singing voice at a navy relief show, Gomer develops a severe case of stage fright that leaves him with laryngitis. He can't talk, let alone sing.

The turning point comes when a despondent Gomer sits on the steps of the Lincoln Memorial and is approached by a park ranger who encourages him to tell him his sob story.

After hearing it, the ranger tells him, "You know what, friend, when I first sat down here I felt sorry for you. But

A security guard (John Gibson) gives Gomer a pep talk in "The Show Must Go On" (Nov. 3, 1967).

I'm not anymore. I'm really not. The people I feel sorry for are the people who are counting on you. Sergeant Carter, the audience—they're the ones you're letting down."

Gomer tries to explain how he is frightened, and the ranger points to Lincoln's statue.

"Now you take him there. He had a lot more to worry about than facing an audience. He had great decisions to make and he must have been frightened many a time. But he didn't let that stop him from doing what he had to do."

Gomer still tries to justify his fear by calling Lincoln a great man and saying, "I'm no hero."

The ranger replies, "You know what I think a hero is? A hero is a man doing the job he has to do the best he knows how."

After he leaves, Gomer starts reciting the Emancipation Proclamation, until slowly, his full voice returns. He belts out a short refrain, and it's off to the navy show to give a rousing rendition of "The Impossible Dream."

No one could belt out "The Impossible Dream" the way Jim Nabors could. The United States Marine Corps Band played themselves in the DC-based episode "The Show Must Go On" (Nov. 3, 1967).

Friendly Freddy was a recurring character on the show who really deserved more airtime. That way he could have sold more shoddy merchandise.

One time he actually sold Gomer a ring that was worth something. In "Friendly Freddy Strikes Again" (Dec. 1, 1967), he accidentally sells the expensive ring to Gomer who gives it to Lou Ann. Now Freddy must try to break the couple up in an effort to get the ring back.

Let it be said, "Clothes make the man." Sid Melton, Frank Sutton, and Jim Nabors in "Friendly Freddy, Gentleman's Tailor" (April 12, 1968).

The shady con artist would close the season in "Friendly Freddy, the Gentleman's Tailor" (April 12, 1968).

Larry Storch of *F Troop* and Borscht Belt fame was a guest in a memorable fourth-season outing titled "Wild Bull of the Pampas" (Dec. 15, 1967).

He played a Latin American general who comes to America to observe the Marine Corps in order to help in leading his own troops.

Manuel Cortez has a hot temper (despite what he says to the contrary) and Gomer seems to be the only one he takes a liking to. That is except for Bunny, in a future visit.

Comedic genius Larry Storch guests as "Wild Bull of the Pampas" (Dec. 15, 1967).

Jerry Van Dyke was another guest in 1968, a man very good at playing someone with very little talent. He had perfected the loser prototype on his brother's show as Rob Petrie's brother Stacey.

Jerry had little luck on television as a headliner, winning infamous razzies as the star of *My Mother, the Car* (1965–1966).

It would be several years, a virtual lifetime in television, before Jerry Van Dyke would be a regular on a hit series.

That moment came with his role as Luther Van Damme on *Coach* (1989–1997).

On a side note, Jerry Van Dyke was best man at Ronnie Schell's wedding, a marriage that has lasted more than fifty years to date. Maybe he wasn't such a jinx after all.

The fourth season and next to last for *Gomer Pyle, U.S.M.C.* solidified Jim's love of performing, and that

Jerry Van Dyke in his only Gomer Pyle *guest shot: "Gomer and the Nightclub Comic" (March 22, 1968).*

meant more than performing as the lovable country goofball who first brought him fame.

Singing was foremost on his mind. Was it possible to leave Gomer Pyle behind and pursue a somewhat different career?

That was a burning question for Jim Nabors throughout the Summer '68. Another season of his successful sitcom loomed, but he was about to make a momentous decision, one he would never regret.

Jim Nabors was poised to become the all-around entertainer he had always dreamed about being.

(12)
NOTABLE OTHERS

They are the oft-unsung heroes of television dramas and sitcoms. They toil from show to show, and if lucky, become a semi-regular or land a recurring role on one of the shows in which they appear.

Forrest Compton could be considered one of the lucky ones over his roughly forty-eight-year career. He was born in Reading, Pennsylvania on Sept. 25, 1925, and passed away April 4, 2020, sadly just before the release of this book.

Had his fortunes played out differently, he may have found his fame as a soap actor. He was in at least six—the most remembered as attorney Mike Karr in *The Edge of Night* (1956–1984).

Compton joined the show in 1972 and remained until it ended in 1984. By this time, fans had grown accustomed to his also being Lieutenant Colonel Edward Gray on *Gomer Pyle, U.S.M.C.*

Gray was stern, commanding as he should have been, not much on smiling, and mostly all military. One character who seemed to break through the veneer was Gomer Pyle. He had that effect on people, and Gray usually sided with Pyle over Carter.

Watch closely a couple of the first-season, black-and-white episodes in which Compton plays Captain Brinson. It would not be long before he returned semi-regularly as Colonel Gray.

Forrest Compton as Colonel Ed Gray.

The reappearance of an actor in a different role happened frequently in sixties' television. He was an unnamed colonel in "Officer Candidate Gomer Pyle" (Feb. 19, 1965), and debuted as Colonel Gray in "Gomer Makes the Honor Guard" (March 5, 1965).

By Season 2, he starts becoming a frustrated witness to some of the shenanigans that go on at Camp Henderson. In "Gomer Untrains a Dog" (Oct. 15, 1965) Gomer takes a trained and vicious guard dog named Killer and tames him down to more of a pussycat named Lemley Gilbert. We learn Gray is a dog man.

It is more apparent in "A Dog is a Dog" (Jan. 12, 1968), in which Carter and Pyle are asked to dog sit the colonel's prized pet, who promptly gets lost.

The two are dumbfounded and round up three look-alike dogs that are not the colonel's beloved pet. He knows exactly what is going on and lets them hang in the wind for a while before the big reveal.

Colonel Gray gets the scoop on his beloved pet in "A Dog is a Dog" (Jan. 22, 1968).

Other than *The Edge of Night* and *Gomer Pyle, U.S.M.C.*, Forrest Compton never had another regular role until he played Mr. Emerson on some episodes of the NBC drama *Ed* (2000–2004).

He was in four episodes of *Hogan's Heroes* and was reunited with his Gomer co-star Ted Bessell on an episode of *That Girl* (1966–1971), titled "Write is Wrong" (Nov. 6, 1969).

Forrest Compton's work throughout the sixties and seventies is extensive. He can be seen in episodes of *The Twilight Zone* (1959–1964), *77 Sunset Strip* (1958–1964), *My Three Sons* (1960–1972), and an early and quite forgotten series called *The Troubleshooters* (1959–1960), about unusual events at construction sites starring Keenan Wynn and Bob Mathias.

One of those episodes of *The Troubleshooters* featured an early appearance by Dan Blocker in the same year he started as Hoss on *Bonanza* (1959–1972).

Forrest Compton retired from acting and went back to live in Reading, Pennsylvania with wife Jeanne Sementini whom he married in 1975.

His last film role was in the Christopher Walken film *McBain* (1991).

He appeared in forty-one episodes of *Gomer Pyle, USMC*.

Another notable—well, ac-tu-ally, one of the most popular characters on *Gomer Pyle, U.S.M.C.*—was a tone-deaf lounge singer named Lou Ann Poovie. Played by blonde, voluptuous Elizabeth MacRae, she provided a steady girl for Gomer.

Elizabeth MacRae came onto the show and would eventually play Jim Nabors' girlfriend.

Having a steady didn't keep him from the monster movies and *Ma and Pa Kettle* pictures however. Luckily his and Lou Ann's tastes were similar.

Her take on "That Old Black Magic" was clearly inspired by the Marilyn Monroe version from the movie *Bus Stop* (1956). Both singers' characters were sultry and oozing sexuality, but couldn't sing worth a lick.

Monroe had practiced constantly on her hillbilly accent for the role of Chérie, whose performance wins her the unwanted affections of cowboy Bo, played by Don Murray.

Lou Ann found suitors in Vince Carter and Duke Slater. Both tried to win her over by promising fame and fortune. It was sensible Gomer

"Lou Ann Poovie Sings Again" (Feb. 22, 1967).

who made her see the light, which was the reality she wasn't cut out to be a singer.

Elizabeth MacRae was a Southern girl, having grown up in Fayetteville, North Carolina. It was a warm, inviting place to which she would return when she tired of the Hollywood scene.

Her film work began in the early sixties. Her first film was *Love in a Goldfish Bowl* (1961), followed up by the just as easily forgettable *Everything's Ducky* (1961).

In 1964, she voiced Ladyfish, in the partly animated Don Knotts film *The Incredible Mr. Limpet*. This would be her last film for ten years until *The Conversation* (1974), an Oscar-nominated film starring Gene Hackman.

Television was her forte. Before Gomer came along, she did episodic work on many hit series. And before she was Gomer's steady, she played April on *Gunsmoke* as girlfriend to Festus Hagan.

So, Gomer was an upgrade!

In real life she married actor and screenwriter Nedrick Young in 1965. Alas, it was to be a short marriage, for he died of a massive coronary in 1968.

Young was blacklisted in the fifties and often wrote under the pseudonym of Nathan E. Douglas. It was as Douglas he won an Oscar, along with co-author Harold Jacob Smith, for their screenplay for *The Defiant Ones*.

Nedrick Young wrote four screenplays. The others were *Jailhouse Rock (1957)*, Inherit *the Wind* (1960), and the ABC-TV movie *Shadow on the Land* (1968), which aired in December after his untimely death.

Blacklisted people in show business lived through an enormous amount of stress. Imagine being singled out for any particular beliefs and banned from working in your trade. The long-term results surely caused health issues.

In Nedrick Young's situation it would seem apparent.

Shadow on the Land dealt a little with these issues. It won praise for its portrait of a United States president overseeing a fascist, totalitarian regime with a resistance movement rising against it.

In 1969, Elizabeth MacRae remarried, to Charles Halsey, the same year *Gomer Pyle, U.S.M.C.* went off the air. Lou Ann's last show was "Friendly Freddy's Computer" (Feb. 14, 1969).

Although there were ten episodes left in the series, Lou Ann's disappearance was never explained.

The character's departure mirrored her later leaving the nostalgia events scene in the mid-2010's, but there was no real mystery. She simply wanted to fade into the limelight quietly and enjoy her golden years in Fayetteville.

One final trivia note before leaving this section: Elizabeth MacRae played a character called Bunny in a 1962 episode of *The Untouchables*. No reports on whether or not anyone called her Miss Bunny.

What *of* our beloved Bunny? To say she was Vince Carter's long-suffering girlfriend would be an understatement.

"Lou Ann on the line . . ."

Barbara Stuart as Bunny, mulling things over.

She was loyal to him, but a pretty gal could obviously turn his head, if only momentarily.

Carter feared commitment. He once had a nightmare of marrying Bunny, in which Gomer appeared at every turn.

She was his steady and played excellently by Barbara Stuart, who was born in Paris, Illinois on Jan. 3, 1930 as Barbara McNeese and raised in nearby Hume.

Bunny appears in twenty-one episodes of *Gomer Pyle, U.S.M.C.* The number seems a modest amount for an important character. Her average of episodes was five per season, with the actress only playing in four episodes during Season 4.

Barbara Stuart first guest-starred as Hannah Troy, the Dragon Lady.

Her TV career began as a secretary named Bessie on the syndicated television version of the popular radio program *The Great Gildersleeve*.

Feature films were never her forte, but guest role after guest role on TV shows was. Her obituary noted she had eighty credits on her acting roster.

We know her first time on *Gomer Pyle, U.S.M.C.* was as the Dragon Lady. Had Bunny not been written in as Carter's girlfriend, he may have remained a callous cad when it came to women. She was a calming influence on the hyperactive Sarge.

He knew he had best behave around Bun or she would let him have it!

She could have left sunny California and been treated like royalty in South America had she accepted General Cortez's advances.

Barbara Stuart was made a regular, playing Miss Bunny.

She liked Gomer, even though his problematic life often caused problems with her and Vince's dating life. Through her influence, he warmed up even more toward his most troublesome private.

In 1967, Barbara Stuart guest-starred on the short-lived CBS series *Mr. Terrific* (1966–1967) where she met nightclub comic and singer Dick Gautier. The two were married the same year, and the marriage lasted until 1979.

Together, they appeared on the daytime game show *Tattletales* (1973–1977). He is remembered for playing Hymie the robot on the Don Adams spy sitcom *Get Smart!* (1965–1970).

Barbara Stuart was also a guest on *Batman* (1966–1968), playing henchwoman to The Puzzler in a fun-filled crime caper. Years later, her husband Dick Gautier would play Batman in a TV commercial, when Adam West refused at a time he was trying to distance himself from the Caped Crusader role.

She died on May 19, 2011. William Grimes called her "a familiar if not famous face on television."

In later years, Barbara Stuart was often confused with another actress named Maxine Stuart. Maxine played on the soap *The Young and the Restless* (1973–present).

At the time of her death, Barbara Stuart had retired to Utah to be near family.

If anyone was ever looking for the perfect person whose "face is familiar, but I can't quite place the name," look no further than Allan Melvin. For sixteen episodes of *Gomer Pyle, U.S.M.C.*, he was Staff Sergeant Charlie Hacker, who ran the mess hall like a tight ship. Hacker took no guff. His main goal in life besides running an efficient kitchen was to one-up Vince Carter.

The wonderfully gifted character actor Allan Melvin as Sgt. Charlie Hacker.

Melvin was born in Kansas City, Missouri on Feb. 18, 1923, but was raised in New York City by his grandparents. In early adulthood, he went to work for NBC radio in the sound effects department. Dreams of show business filled his head, as did marriage.

Allan married Amalia Faustina Sestero in March, 1944. While in the sound effects department at NBC, he auditioned to do a comedy act at a nightclub and got the job. He was able to parlay this into an appearance on the popular (and often star-making) *Arthur Godfrey's Talent Scouts* (1946–1958).

Phil Silvers must have been watching and was "glad he seen it!" For that appearance led to Allan Melvin being cast as Corporal Henshaw on Silvers' show, now known as *The Phil Silvers Show*, but was originally called *You'll Never Get Rich*.

Playing Henshaw cemented Allan Melvin as a reliable player and as a loud and abrasive one. After the series left the air he was seen frequently playing these types of roles.

"Okay, Let's hear it for Henshaw!"

Sheldon Leonard and Aaron Ruben liked his work and he spent a great deal of the sixties working for them. He was in eight episodes of *The Andy Griffith Show* and eight more in *The Dick Van Dyke Show*.

On *Griffith*, he was once a prison escapee, a burly store owner, and a peddler who gets run off by Barney. He and Knotts were good as foes. One of Melvin's characters once promised to beat the tar out of the deputy if he ever caught him out of uniform.

Barney's solution was to never take the uniform off!

In addition to so many guest shots, Allan Melvin was also a prolific voice actor. His signature voice work came with the cartoon *Magilla Gorilla* (1964–1966) in which he was the voice of Magilla.

Charlie Hacker was a later add-on to *Gomer Pyle, U.S.M.C.* He and Vince liked making bets, and Gomer was often the unknowing pawn in these wagers.

A sly devil, this Hacker, he was always watching . . . and from his keen observation, knew just what it was about Pyle that got on Carter's last nerve.

In the fifth-season episode, "Come Blow Your Top" (Nov. 29, 1968), Hacker bets Carter fifty bucks he cannot go twenty-four hours without losing his temper.

Hacker and Carter trying to one-up each other in their dress blues.

That's not a wager most people who knew Carter would want to bet against. At one point, Carter becomes so frustrated that he drives out into the middle of nowhere to scream.

After the *Pyle* series ended, Allan Melvin went into another signature role, and perhaps it is his best-known one. He played Sam the butcher, boyfriend to Alice, the Brady's housekeeper extraordinaire on *The Brady Bunch*.

In the seventies, he joined the cast of *All in the Family* as the Bunkers' next-door neighbor, Barney Hefner. Barney wasn't an important character until the series spun off into *Archie Bunker's Place* (1979–1983) and he was one of the regulars at the bar.

Melvin continued to do voice-overs for cartoons. This was his only work after *Archie Bunker's Place* went off the air.

He died of cancer on Jan. 17, 2008 and was survived by his wife. On looking back on his career and speaking specifically about *The Phil Silvers Show*, she told Associated Press, "I think the camaraderie of all those guys made it such a pleasant place to work. They were so relaxed."

The same could have been said of his time on *Gomer Pyle, U.S.M.C.* Well, there may have been one hotheaded sergeant who never seemed very relaxed!

Howard Weston "Ted" Bessell was classically trained to be a musician. He was born in Flushing, New York on March 20, 1935, and by age twelve had performed a piano recital onstage at Carnegie Hall.

His thoughts drifted more toward acting, and he trained under famed acting coach Sanford Meisner at the Neighborhood Playhouse. By the late fifties, he was working as a page at ABC to supplement his meager income.

A couple of early roles for Ted Bessell were a panelist on the 1962 game show *Who*

Ted Bessell and Jim Nabors made an entertaining team, seen here in "Third Finger, Left Loaf" (Sept. 24, 1965).

Do You Trust? hosted by Johnny Carson, and on Dick Clark's Saturday night rock 'n' roll show.

While in the touring company of *Look Homeward, Angel* in California, he started auditioning for movies. Though the parts were small, he enhanced the films *The Outsider* (1961), *Lover Come Back* (1963), and *Captain Newman, M.D.* (1963) with his presence.

In 1962, he found a job as a regular on the series *It's a Man's World* (1962–1963). Co-Starring Glenn Corbett, Randy Boone, and Michael Burns, the series focused on a group of young men living on a houseboat while engaged in their main pursuit—that of the opposite sex.

Corbett's character was trying to raise his younger brother Burns around his good-time buddies who weren't the best influence.

The show was considered ahead of its time because of the generation gap issues it dealt with. Many critics believed if given more time, *It's a Man's World* could have been a success, but the ratings would not wait.

The idea was revived somewhat in 1976 for the very short-lived ABC series *The San Pedro Beach Bums*.

Hold on to that ring at all costs!

Where to go but the military? Ted became a regular on *Gomer Pyle, U.S.M.C.* in 1966. His first appearance was as a character named Jim Purcell, but after that episode, he became Frankie Lombardi forever.

He was just in time for the shipboard antics in the three-story navy arc. He takes Gomer home to meet his family in "Arrivederci Gomer" (Jan. 21, 1966), and Gomer sings a love song to Frankie's sister who is engaged, more or less, to another fellow.

Bessell appeared in twenty episodes of the show all together, actually more than the other notables being covered here. For a while, he was doing double duty after winning the role of Donald

Hollinger, boyfriend to Ann Marie in the series *That Girl*.

The role was destined to make him, if not a household name, a household face. From the very first episode in which he mistakenly believes Ann is in danger, he introduces himself by accidentally bashing her in the head with his briefcase.

"Call me Captain Dumb-Dumb," he tells her.

She was more comfortable calling him Donald. She rarely called him Don. He became her steady boyfriend and later agent, much to the chagrin of her father, Lew Marie.

Ted Bessell with Gigi Perreau and Lillian Adams in "Arrivederci Gomer" (Jan. 21, 1966).

Had *That Girl* gone another season past 1971, the couple was slated for a lavish on-air wedding. A wedding on a long-running series was often designed as a ratings boost, though most failed to help their respective series in the long run.

When Tony and Jeannie married on *I Dream of Jeannie*, it took a bit of the magic away.

Bessell remained with *Gomer Pyle, U.S.M.C.* until the very last episode "Goodbye Camp Henderson, Hello Sergeant Carter" (May 2, 1969).

Besides a few episodes as another boyfriend, this time to Mary Tyler Moore on her popular series *The Mary Tyler Moore Show*, Ted Bessell won the distinction of starring in one of the "worst" series of that time period.

Me and the Chimp (1973) was about a dentist who gains

Bessell and buddies back in the barracks.

a newfound, and at first, unwanted best friend when his family begs him successfully to let them keep a chimp named Buttons.

For thirteen episodes, Buttons causes havoc in the Reynolds household. He winds up helping the son's basketball team in one episode, draws a longer line on a road map in another, and strands the family in a ghost town.

Bessell insisted on top billing above his co-star and reportedly hated Buttons with a passion. Hey, the primate got all the laughs. He learned as Ronald Reagan did in *Bedtime for Bonzo* (1951).

Reagan said of this film, "I fought a losing battle with a scene stealer with a built-in edge—he was a chimpanzee!"

In one scene, the chimp, whose real name was Peggy, grabs the future president's necktie—and refusing to let go—nearly strangles him.

Bessell and Buttons had no such near catastrophes. By December 1973, they parted company. The actress who played Bessell's daughter on the show, Kami Cotler, went on to play Elizabeth on the long-running CBS staple *The Waltons*.

Bessell's last two acting attributes of any note were starring in the brief summer 1980 series *Wild About Harry*, in which he played a callous sportswriter fired from every job and on his last chance with a San Francisco paper. Harry was very unlike Ted, and audiences did not accept it.

Ted as Frankie Lombardi, making Gomer's mouth water with descriptions of Mama's cannoli and chicken cacciatore.

Lasting even less time was *Hail to the Chief*, which only made it on air from April 9, 1985 to May 21, 1985. Here Patty Duke played the first woman president and Bessell was her husband, the First Gentleman, so to speak.

It was produced by Tony Thomas, Marlo's brother and was intended to be a zany satire in the same vein as *Soap* (1977–1981), but viewers didn't think so, and it was quickly impeached.

Not much acting followed for Ted Bessell. He found a new "direction" as a director. Mainly he honed his new craft with episodes of the Fox series, *The Tracey Ullman Show* (1987–1991).

At the time of his untimely death at age sixty-one on Oct. 6, 1996, Ted Bessell was preparing to be honored with an all-star tribute at the Museum of Television and Radio History, slated for Oct. 11.

He is buried at Woodlawn Memorial Cemetery in Santa Monica, California.

Brooklyn-born Sid Melton (1917) made his stage debut in a touring company of a show called *See My Lawyer*, and in 1939 got his first film role in *Shadow of the Thin Man* as a shifty character called Fingers.

He went to work for low-budget Lippert Pictures in 1949. Some of their movies were shot in less than a week.

Sid Melton as Friendly Freddy.

Melton played comic relief in most of those he appeared in. He was in the slightly bigger-budgeted *On the Town* (1949) with Frank Sinatra and Gene Kelly.

In the early fifties, he was Ichabod Mudd, sidekick to Captain Midnight in the kiddie show *Captain Midnight* (1954–1956).

He found security in playing Danny Thomas' agent on his show. Sheldon Leonard liked the squirrely and slick persona of Sid Melton and started casting him in a lot of his shows he produced.

Sixties television audiences of course, remember him for two significant roles. As inept carpenter Alf Monroe who is doing more damage than good to the Douglas' farmhouse on *Green Acres*, he works alongside with brother Ralph, who is a girl.

And we cheered him (or jeered) him as two-bit conman Friendly Freddy on *Gomer Pyle, U.S.M.C.* With only four appearances, the character is still fondly remembered by fans.

He sold mostly defective goods, and Pyle and Sgt. Carter were his two biggest patsies. He could never remember Gomer's name,

"No, no, no, Lyle, I mean Peel ... I mean Homer ..."

often calling him something like "Homer Lyle."

He operated out of the trunk of his car and was a pure depiction of a traveling salesman with absolutely no scruples.

Most of his later work was in TV commercials and an occasional movie, mostly ones designed for the drive-in circuit.

He died of pneumonia on November 2, 2011. He was ninety-four. Melton was interred at Mount Sinai Memorial Cemetery in L.A. As Friendly Freddy, his deals were not the best, but one knew whenever he showed up—laughs would follow.

William Christopher as Pvt. Lester Hummell.

William Christopher, the diminutive and witty performer will forever be most associated with his thirteen years playing priest Father Mulcahy. He first played the role on *M*A*S*H* (1972 – 1983), then on its short-lived spin-off *After-M*A*S*H* (1983–1985).

He acquired the role after the original actor named George Morgan was let go after the pilot was filmed.

For sixteen episodes, he was Private Lester Hummel on *Gomer Pyle, U.S.M.C.* Hummel was an easygoing member of the platoon, and at times a voice of reason, whether listened to or not.

He can also be found playing alongside Don Knotts in the comedy western *The Shakiest Gun in the West* (1968), and the film *With Six You Get Eggroll* (1968). That's memorable, because it pairs him in a scene with his future *M*A*S*H** costar Jamie Farr, five years before they hit Korea courtesy of CBS.

During the nineties, the Evanston, Illinois-born Christopher toured in a stage production of *The Odd Couple* with Jamie Farr.

William Christopher died in 2016 at the age of eighty-eight.

Special mention should also be made of the two appearances on *Gomer Pyle, U.S.M.C.* by the vivacious Joyce Jameson (September 26, 1932–January 16, 1987). She is well remembered as one of the Fun Girls on *The Andy Griffith Show* and making problems for Andy and Barney.

Joyce Jameson, a fun girl having fun in "Vacation in Vegas" (March 11, 1968).

Jameson played Skippy, the giggly one of the two. Daphne was played by gravelly-voiced Jean Carson, whose signature greeting was "Hello Doll!"

Watch for Joyce Jameson in these two *Gomer Pyle* episodes: "Vacation in Vegas" (March 11, 1966), and "The Return of Monroe" (Oct. 18, 1968).

Speaking of Monroe, he was Lou Ann's boyfriend from back home who ultimately lost out to Gomer. He was played by famed clarinetist Med Flory who had been in bands with Claude Thornhill and Woody Herman. While music was what he enjoyed most and is best known for, Flory's work in sixties' television is quite prolific. He seems to turn up everywhere.

Med Flory is "Go, go, go!" in "The Return of Monroe" (Oct. 18, 1968).

Roy Stuart was excellent as Corporal Boyle.

Roy Stuart (1927–2005) was not the first Corporal Boyle, but is the best remembered. He was born in the Bronx and started his career in nightclubs.

Earlier, Richard Sinatra, cousin to Frank, had been Boyle. The character was a sounding board of sensibility for Sergeant Carter, even though Carter did not like to listen to reason.

Stuart can be found in many of the signature shows of the sixties and seventies. He appeared in the second, third, and fourth seasons of *Gomer Pyle, U.S.M.C.*, but was gone completely when Duke Slater returned and became the corporal assigned to Carter.

One of his later funny turns was as a reporter named Don Martin in a *Sanford and Son* episode where Fred lies in a hospital bed under witness protection, ready to identify notorious mobster Mr. Big.

Stuart belonged to a group of actors who performed at Theatre West and dearly loved performing on stage. He especially loved being in *The Sunshine Boys*.

Boyle's life beyond the military is not covered. It is a few episodes in before we even find out his first name is Chuck. He was mainly there to provide a companion to Carter, a person who tried to be a friend more than a subordinate.

He was not as good a mediator between the sergeant and Pyle as Duke, but he tried. Fans liked his portrayal, and

Classic poses—Frank Sutton and Roy Stuart.

Corporal Boyle can be considered a significant part of the overall success of the series.

Roy Stuart died in 2005 of cancer and is buried in Eden Memorial Park Cemetery in Mission Hills.

Konstantin Stanislavski once coined a phrase when he said, "There are no small parts, only small actors."

Each actor or actress who contributed to *Gomer Pyle, U.S.M.C.* helped in their own way to make it a success. It's true that if you start adding up names, you will find a healthy list of those who were also on Andy Griffith's show.

Then look closer, and you will find them on many other series of the day.

We need players like this today. There is a warmth and comfort in seeing these people and recognizing their faces and voices.

They have become friends.

(13)
SEASON FIVE

Final seasons are bittersweet. After all, we are leaving friends behind. Without resolution, we are left to believe the characters we have grown to love and sometimes not love so much, stay frozen in perpetual time. Imagine the castaways on *Gilligan's Island*. Thank goodness a TV movie aired, *Rescue from Gilligan's Island* (1978), eleven years after the tropical sitcom was levied to give a few more years to *Gunsmoke*.

When it came to *Gomer Pyle, U.S.M.C.*, Jim Nabors took a cue from other greats in the entertainment field. Andy Griffith had said that he would only commit to doing his own show for five seasons, and he kept his word. Dick Van Dyke knew at the end of his fifth year on the air it was time to bow out.

Ending a series early might be a bummer for fans, but it does give producers and writers a chance to wrap things up tidily. Mary Tyler Moore had an emotional end to her seventies' series.

Bob Newhart went out with a doozy of an ending on his eighties' series. It proved, as Shakespeare said, "Dreams are acts of pure imagination." Gomer and gang also had a resolution of sorts with the last episode, but before we get to that, there is a whole season to ponder.

It kicked off with the marvelously written and played "Car for Sale" (Sept. 27, 1968). Once again Hacker and Carter are at it, as in at each other's throats. Vince reneges on selling his car to good ol' Charlie, and sells it to Gomer instead.

Sergeant Hacker had already put a plan in motion earlier to make his buddy think the 1958 Dodge Coronet is getting bad gas mileage, by draining the gas every night.

It is a hilarious episode filled with laughs and surprises, and ends appropriately with a bang.

The second Season 5 episode was "Corporal Duke" (Oct. 4, 1968), which marked the triumphant return of Ronnie Schell as Duke Slater, now a corporal.

One of the winners of the season turned out to be a beauty called "The Booty Prize" (Oct. 11, 1968).

One platoon is going to win it—a bronzed boot, the symbol of inadequacy among all platoons. Sergeant Carter does not want the distinction of winning the boot once again.

He makes the mistake of leaving the boot with Gomer to shine. While the boot symbolizes failure as a whole, there is still a fascination attached to it.

Who wouldn't want to try on a bronze boot?

First Gomer, then Carter, then Hacker ... and it isn't an easy boot to remove. Using the freezer is a grand idea if one doesn't get caught, as happens here.

It would be interesting to find out if this particular episode was purely the imagination of writers, or if there is a tradition of some similarity in the Marines where the worst platoon is rewarded by such a prize.

Carter explains the dubious honor of a certain trophy in his usual laid-back way in "The Booty Prize" (Oct. 11, 1968).

"Get it off!" pleads Hacker, after getting the boot stuck on his foot, too.

There are also the wonderful Hollywood-based episodes. By the seventh episode, "A Marriage of Convenience" (Nov. 15, 1968), we see the progression of Gomer actually becoming more savvy in worldly ways than Sergeant Carter.

A movie star named Pola Prevost finds her visa is about to expire, and she requires a husband fast! She latches on to gullible Gomer—but not so fast—Gomer isn't quite that gullible. After all, that's not how things are done back home, and she hasn't even met his momma yet.

Nita Talbot plays the star fabulously in a role she always perfected. Next victim, i.e., potential groom, is none other than Sergeant Vincent Carter, who falls for it.

Nita Talbot as Pola Prevost in "A Marriage of Convenience" (Nov. 15, 1968).

Gomer really steps in and saves the day here and does it in a way so Carter never finds out. And good old Duke; he is all for letting the sergeant hang here, and find a Dear John letter on his pillow some morning.

Jesse White played Pola's agent. He would later find work as the exasperated Maytag repairman in TV commercials.

"A Star is Not Born" (Nov. 22, 1968) presents us with the filming of a scene for the movie *Leathernecks of the Air*. Vince has one line . . . that's right, one line: "Okay, let's hear it for Henshaw!"

Sgt. Hacker (Allan Melvin) and Cpl. Jensen (Victor Brant) up to no good in "Come Blow Your Top" (Nov. 24, 1968).

He flubs it time and time again.

Once again, Gomer saves the shoot, but poor old Sarge looks a bit embarrassed as well as incapacitated by the solution. Watch for a guest turn by Jamie Farr sans dress as one of the set people.

The next one, "Come Blow Your Top" (Nov. 29, 1968), has them back at Camp Henderson. Carter and Hacker are betting again. This time

Hacker bets him he cannot go twenty-four hours without losing his temper.

With Gomer always lurking around, that will be a hard wager for Carter to win.

What to do, but drive out to the vast wilderness and scream your head off.

"A Little Chicken Soup Wouldn't Hurt" (Dec. 6, 1968) marks a rare appearance on network television by Broadway actress Molly Picon. She plays a lonely old woman befriended by Pyle in the park. Her son pays little or no attention to her and she longs for someone to cook for.

Soon, Gomer invites all his buddies to come to her house and enjoy some delicious home cooking.

Molly had been a star in the Yiddish theater, and at the height of her fame in the twenties, had her own theater. Her other notable TV work was a recurring role as Mrs. Bronson on *Car 54, Where are You?* (1961 – 1963).

She was also on the NBC soap Somerset (1970 – 1976) and Natalie's grandmother on *The Facts of Life* (1979–1986).

Ironically, her first movie role with substantial screen time was *Come Blow Your Horn* (1958) with Frank Sinatra. The title was slightly changed for the title of the previous *Gomer Pyle, U.S.M.C.* episode.

Molly Picon was also the matchmaker in the film version of *Fiddler on the Roof* (1971).

Broadway star Molly Picon made a rare appearance in "A Little Chicken Soup Wouldn't Hurt" (Dec. 6, 1968).

"Two on a Bench" (Jan. 3, 1969) kicked off the new year in style. Gomer sees from a newspaper Joey is reading, that his old buddy Ellery Lewis is in town.

Ellery (Glenn Ash) is now known as Moose Lewis and is a popular fullback for the Boston Bulldogs football franchise. Coincidentally,

Sergeant Carter at the same time is desperately trying to score tickets for Sunday's big game.

Gomer receives a call from an old friend on the phone in Carter's duty hut. It is Moose (Ellery) inviting him to come see him, and later he invites him to sit on the bench Sunday at the big game.

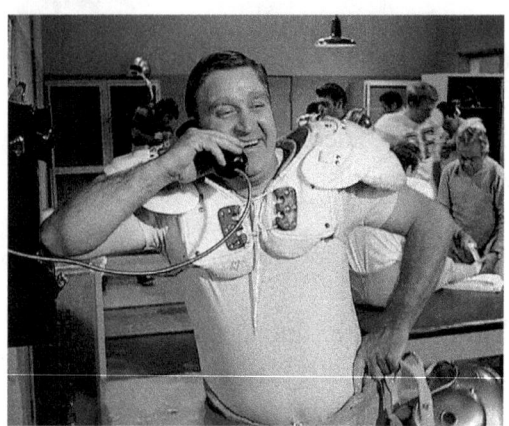

Ellery "Moose" Lewis (Glenn Ash) extends a special invitation to ol' buddy Gomer in "Two on a Bench" (Jan. 3, 1969).

Carter is too busy to take in what Pyle is trying to explain to him. He has to have a ticket to the game.

It finally dawns on Vince, while he is tossing and turning, trying to sleep, what Gomer actually said. He goes to a slumbering Pyle to get verification that he heard right.

"Moose Lewis? Moose Lewis is a friend of yours?"

Of course, he is. He and Gomer worked together back at the fillin' station in Mayberry, and he once knitted Gomer a pair of socks that he wore for two years.

Not two years straight, mind you.

More complications follow when Moose suffers a temporary head injury during practice, and it lasts long enough to convince Carter that Pyle's story is full of holes.

Carter is very upset. Pyle swore on the Marine emblem that he knew Moose Lewis.

As soon as the footballer regains his senses he straightens it out as Carter is still anxiously trying to get a ticket

Gomer and his sergeant with a disoriented Moose Lewis.

to the big game. He has even resorted to calling notorious scalper Ziggy.

Again, come game day, there are more problems. There is just one pass and it is for Gomer Pyle only. Well, Ziggy is patrolling the crowd, looking for a sucker. Here comes Vince Carter.

We know all will end well, don't we? Carter makes it on the bench with Gomer, but let's just say he does not quite see the whole game. He doesn't see much of anything for a couple of hours.

"Get the phone will ya?"

"Two on the Bench" is such a terrific episode. It is absolute proof of the series improvement, here at the mid-season-point beginning of its final year's run.

It satisfies right up to its "smashup" of an ending.

One of the highlights from "Two on the Bench" is a duet of a novelty song called "You Can't Have Your Kate and Edith Too" sung by Jim Nabors and Glenn Ash.

It is a cute little ditty which—fair warning—might be cut from some televised showings. In researching this book, the episode which was posted on YouTube does include it.

"You Can't Have Your Kate and Edith Too" was written by Bobby Braddock and Curly Putman for the Statler Brothers in 1967. It is included on Johnny Cash's Folsom Prison album.

Since Pyle and Lewis haven't seen each other for nearly five years and this is a song they used to sing at work, there may be some argument as to who really wrote it.

Gomer and Moose (Jim Nabors and Glenn Ash).

For how could they have sung a song that wasn't even written for another four years?

Glenn Ash was a corporal in the air force in the late forties, who could not only play a mean guitar, but needed to hear a song only a few times before he could play all the chords. He was discovered by Don Knotts and he soon found work on television, first on *The Hollywood Palace* (1964–1970) in 1968.

Besides *Gomer Pyle, U.S.M.C.*, he also appeared on *The Leslie Uggams Show* (1969), *Mayberry RFD* (1968–1971), *The Glenn Campbell Goodtime Hour* (1969–1972), and *Petticoat Junction* (1963–1970).

He was also on episodes of *M*A*S*H** (1972–1983), *Hart to Hart* (1979–1984), and *Rags to Riches* (1987–1988).

Ash was also a regular on Andy Griffith's second series, *The New Andy Griffith Show* (1971), but only appeared in two episodes before CBS pulled the plug.

The team doctor is played by Jerry Hausner who was Ricky Ricardo's agent on *I Love Lucy* (1951–1957).

One would think Gomer learned his lesson about the dos and don'ts of life-saving with Andy. Yet, in "To Save a Life" (Jan. 31, 1969), we have a virtual replay of this theme.

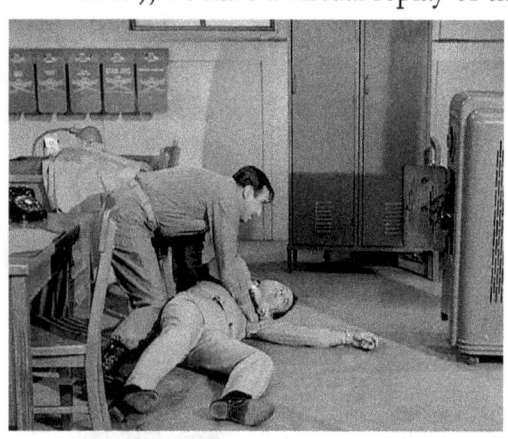

Saving the life of the man who saved his life. "To Save a Life" (Jan. 31, 1969).

Sergeant Carter saves the clumsy private's life, and Gomer tells him he will be forever grateful.

"Nothing's too good for the man who saved my life."

Indeed, he starts waiting on the sergeant hand and foot. There's breakfast in bed, washing and ironing his uniforms, shining his boots, detailing his car (including adjusting the brakes), and Gomer even asks Sergeant Hacker if he can use the mess hall to bake Sergeant Carter some brownies.

All this adulation is driving Carter crazy.

He hits upon the idea that if Gomer were to somehow save his life, then they would be even. No one would owe anyone. But how to pull this off?

"Look," Carter tells Duke, "you come barreling at me in the jeep, and just as you're about to hit me, Pyle pushes me out of the way. What could go wrong?"

Plenty. Carter is almost killed for real. Then he tries pretending to have fallen into a well. Let's just say Gomer is no Lassie when it comes to rescuing people who have fallen into wells.

Carter con-"Vinces" Gomer that they're all even now, while Duke (Ronnie Schell) looks on.

How about gassing himself? Even this doozy of a plan fails. Gomer winds up being the one gassed. Carter can't have Pyle thinking he has saved his life once again.

There are some hilarious scenes in "To Save a Life," even if the feeling we've seen it all before persists.

One of the funniest bits in the episode has Carter taking

At the movies.

Bunny to a low-budget movie titled *Flame of the South Seas*. She remarks he always takes her to movies that are about ten minutes from being on television.

He says Slater personally recommended it, even though what he actually said is, it may be the worst movie of the year.

Guess who else shows up at the movie theater? None other than good ol' Gomer.

There is an ancient Chinese belief that if you save a person's life you are responsible for it. That is the reverse of what Gomer believed.

Either way, life-saving is a good thing, but should be approached with extreme caution—or risk being pestered for life.

Another Season 5 episode that was reworked from another sitcom comes along in "Dynamite Diner" (Feb. 7, 1969). This time the idea derives from an episode of *Car 54, Where Are You?* titled "White Elephant" (Jan. 6, 1963).

Gomer and Lou Ann are on a date one sunny afternoon and neither one seems to know what they want to do with the day. They discover a new diner that is not quite ready for business yet, if it will ever be.

The would-be restaurateurs, Charlie and Herb, are crooks who only rented the place because it shares an adjoining wall with the bank. Their plan is to dynamite through to the vault.

Gomer and Lou Ann want to help the two fellows make a go of the restaurant. They go out and buy more food and decorations. Then they invite the platoon in for a Saturday-night sampling of fried chicken.

Noam Pitlik as Herb admires a one-handed culinary maneuver by Gomer in "Dynamite Diner" (Feb. 7, 1969).

This is the same night as the planned robbery. Charlie figures why not use the restaurant full of noisy Marines as the perfect cover for the sound of the explosion.

As well as dropping a pile of plates. "There go the profits," Charlie says and chuckles.

"Dynamite Diner" is another good example of Gomer, the good Samaritan. No matter how his attempts are sometimes bungled, he is more than likely to change those he encounters and leave them better off for it.

Herb, who has never even fried an egg before, is the first to evolve. He believes they could really go straight and run a legitimate place. Charlie beams as well, when he wears one of the chef's hat Gomer and Lou Ann purchased for them.

When the robbery attempt proves to be a "washout," we are left to believe that possibly Charlie and Herb will reform thanks to Gomer Pyle.

He had that kind of influence.

Charlie was played by Lewis Charles, a veteran character actor who was also on Andy Griffith's show. Herb was played by Noam Pitlik, a prolific guest star on sixties' series who later became a director, winning an Emmy for directing on *Barney Miller*.

Before reaching the final episode for this examination of the last season, let us look at "I'm Always Chasing Gomers" (March 7. 1969).

Carter is developing "Pyle-itis," which includes a major symptom of twitching eye. He tells Slater he has to get away if only for the weekend.

"Where you gonna go Sarge? L.A., Vegas?"

"Wichita."

Yes, Vince believes only a trip back home to see Mom will cure him of being around the irritating Pyle too long.

Without Carter's knowledge, Pyle ends up going with him. If you don't know how this happened, please don't ask.

So, even in Wichita, Carter sees Gomer at every turn.

Lewis Charles played the half of a bank-robbing duo most disinclined to go straight in "Dynamite Diner" (Feb. 7, 1969).

It started with a twitch ... "I'm Always Chasing Gomers" (March 7, 1969).

Pyle needs seventy-two dollars for a flight back to Camp Henderson. He cannot and does not intend for Carter to find out he is in town.

Vince's mom is played by the delightful Kathleen Freeman. She has graced audiences with her face and talent in everything from *Hogan's Heroes* to Jerry Lewis movies.

Mom and her "little Vincie" (Kathleen Freeman with Frank Sutton).

There is nothing better for Mom and son than watching their favorite TV program together, *Roller Derby,* and having a beer. That is, until Gomer looks in the window.

There is also a spooky moment for "little Vincie," who was always afraid of ghosts in the attic, when he spies a ghoulish Pyle in a long nightshirt in that very place.

For an episode this late into a series winding to a close, "I'm Always Chasing Gomers" is a big win. In watching, one would think another season surely loomed.

Alas, it was not to be.

"Goodbye Camp Henderson, Hello Sergeant Carter" (May 2, 1969) was the swan song. The episode consists mostly of flashbacks, with Carter recalling all the heartaches Pyle has caused him and then being reminded how Gomer eventually saved the day.

(14)
VARIETY SHOW

Because singing was Jim Nabors' first love, the thought of doing his own variety show was probably foremost in his mind long before *Gomer Pyle, U.S.M.C.* left the air. A November, 1965 variety special featuring he, Andy Griffith and Don Knotts, had spectacular ratings.

American Motors sponsored a special in 1967 called *Friends and Nabors* with Andy Griffith, Tennessee Ernie Ford, Marilyn Horne and Shirley Jones. Again, the ratings were phenomenal.

There was one more special in the offing. 1968's *Girl Friends and Nabors* was splashy and ended with Jim singing a big band version of Ernest Tubb's "Tomorrow Never Comes."

Our star was also tiring of the grind of memorizing so many lines of dialogue every night. As Gomer, he was in practically every scene.

Jim consulted his agent Dick Linke who told him that if he wanted to try something different, now would be the time. He was never hotter than at the end of Gomer's five-year run.

Jim Nabors cuts loose with Andy Griffith and Don Knotts for his 1965 variety special.

Jim with guests Tennessee Ernie Ford and Andy Griffith on Friends and Nabors *(1967).*

The same time slot was even originally planned for Friday night until CBS picked up the recently canceled *Get Smart!* to give it one more year of life after NBC axed it.

So execs looked to Thursday at 7:00 p.m. Central Time when the popular specials had aired. *The Jim Nabors Hour* debuted on Sept. 25, 1969 to thunderous applause. Andy Griffith was a premiere guest. Perhaps he was Jim's "good luck charm." Good old Don Knotts popped up for a cameo and there was also an up-and-coming singer named Julie Budd who would appear in other Nabors hours.

The debut scored a 26 in the ratings and was the fourth most watched program of the week.

The opening of that episode is a clip often used today when the show is mentioned. As stars from *Gomer Pyle, U.S.M.C.* waltz out onstage in Marine garb to the accompaniment of "If My Friends Could See Me Now," they peel off the outer clothing to reveal tuxedo and evening wear.

This is to say all but Frank Sutton, who quickly runs offstage because all he has on is his undergarments.

1969 was a very good year for the variety show genre. It is a bit hard for audiences of today to imagine how popular these extravaganzas were. The stage work and setting up, plus costumes, was a monumental weekly chore.

Broadway was still considered the epitome of show business. The television variety show was like watching a Broadway production in the comfort of one's own living room.

There was a time when there were so many variety shows on air. Dean Martin,

Variety show time—Ronnie Schell, Jim Nabors, Karen Morrow, and Frank Sutton in the early seventies.

Andy Williams, Glenn Campbell, The Smothers Brothers, as well as Carol Burnett all had late-sixties' winners.

Holidays meant hour-long Christmas specials with the likes of Bing Crosby. Bob Hope did regular variety specials on NBC that always won the ratings for the night.

Yes, Jim Nabors had gambled, and that gamble paid off. *The Jim Nabors Hour* was far removed from *Gomer Pyle, U.S.M.C.* but gave its fans another way to enjoy the performers they had come to cherish.

There was a popular sketch called "The Brothers-In-Law" that featured Jim, Frank, Ronnie, and Karen Morrow. Jim and Frank were Loomis and Harry, the brothers-in-law who ran a rooming house. Ronnie played Audie, a boarder who was often drunk and slid down stairs.

It had great promise and story lines. "The Brothers-in-Law" could very well have been converted into a series of its own, much like Carol Burnett did with *Mama's Family* (1983–1990).

Ronnie Schell as Audie the drunk, udder, er ... under a cow apparently wearing shoes.

The second episode saw the arrival of old friend Carol Burnett. There is a hilarious sketch where Carol plays the wife of the Lone Ranger—Mrs. Lone Ranger—who grows tired of her husband being gone all the time rescuing folks on the prairie.

It's possible she has turned to Tonto (Ronnie Schell) for comfort.

Watch for the opening of the closet and all those silver bullets!

Jim and Carol get to do a grand singing session of roundelays and Frank discusses gunslingers in the Old West. Jim also sings an outstanding version of "I Can't Stop Loving You."

The variety show gave Jim a chance to interact with many show business friends in all-new ways. There has been some discussion among concerned fans as to how much sway he, as star, had in the selection of guests.

Guests for variety shows were usually chosen by producers for promotional reasons or for the sheer star power. However, either those

Variety shows, whether The Jim Nabors Hour *or* The Carol Burnett Show *(here with Carol, Jim, and Vicki Lawrence), packed in Broadway-style production and top guest stars to thrill TV audiences.*

Jim Nabors at the podium: always a class act.

producers knew Jim's mindset to a tee or he did have major influence. A glimpse over the guest list confirms this.

Musical numbers took center stage. There were few other places on television in the late sixties/early seventies where one could find opera stars and Broadway-style performances.

Kate Smith, Glenn Campbell, Bobbie Gentry, Tennessee Ernie Ford, Marilyn Horne, The Jackson 5, Vikki Carr, Minnie Pearl, Kay Starr, Eddy Arnold, Roy Rogers, Dale Evans, Roger Miller, Bobby Goldsboro, Jackie DeShannon, Rick Nelson, and Johnny and June Carter Cash were among the diverse musical guests.

The Jackson 5 opened the second season on Sept. 17, 1970. Instead of doing one of the more R&B-type songs for which they were known, they performed a production number called "Gospel Now."

Their careers were just getting underway, but their domineering father Joe was still everywhere they were, calling the shots. He and Sgt. Carter would quite likely have gotten along.

The second episode of the second season (Sept. 24, 1970) had Carol Burnett back as a woman who finds herself trapped in her bathtub when her finger gets caught in the drain. The finale was set in Paris with a salute to Toulouse-Lautrec and the Paris nightclub scene.

Glenn Campbell was in a Foreign Legion sketch (Oct. 15, 1970). Andy Griffith performed a "Daniel in the Lion's Den" monologue (Oct. 29, 1970). Nabors was hired as an extra in a new Roy Rogers movie (Dec. 10, 1970). Ronnie Schell played newsman Walter Concrete interviewing French sex symbol Brigette Boffo (Totie Fields) in an episode broadcast on Dec. 17, 1970.

Another memorable skit was a spoof of *Cinderella* with Barbara McNair as Cinderella, Jim as Prince Charming, and Frank and Ronnie playing Cinderella's stepsisters.

Jim was able to spoof his old Mayberry mechanic days, playing an inept mechanic in skits with both Joan Rivers and Rock Hudson.

The Hudson appearance was the one that began the stupid tabloid rumors. For the record, there has never been any substantiation of anything other than a working relationship between Nabors and Hudson.

On the January 22, 1970 episode—the gas station sketch—he and Hudson reminisced about growing up in small towns, sang "Don't It Make You Want To Go Home" together. In "The Brothers-In-Law," Rock can get no rest when the family discovers their new boarder is a celebrity.

Since it is highly likely these episodes will never be seen again, we can at least give some descriptions of the excellent "The Brothers-In-Law" sketches.

In one, Harry (Frank Sutton) tries pulling an insurance scam by wearing a neck brace, but honest Loomis (Jim Nabors) is sure to spill the beans.

In others, they try installing an air conditioner, win a raffle for a new car but lose the winning ticket, and Loomis takes a hotel management class then tries to upgrade the boarding house with disastrous results. One show has Loomis renting a room to a traveling circus and its menagerie of animals, and another, a very funny sketch where a chain-smoking Harry tries desperately to kick the habit.

Often, Jim guested on the shows of his guests. He appeared on the shows of Glenn Campbell, Bobby Goldsboro and Johnny Cash.

The last episode of *The Jim Nabors Hour* was broadcast on March 18, 1971 and had no traditional guests. There were the Tony Mordente Dancers, but they were featured on quite a few of the episodes. Jim sang "Danny Boy" and "The Impossible Dream," and a Broadway melody closed it out.

The Jim Nabors Hour became a part of history. There were some reruns into the summer of 1971, but of course, the infamous "rural purge" that fall eliminated, as Pat Buttram said, "Every show that had a tree in it."

Singer Julie Budd today.

Julie Budd was a popular cabaret singer who appeared in many of the episodes. She was born in 1954, and as of this publication date still performs in New York where she lives.

She released a record for MGM records in 1968 called *Child of Plenty*. She was also a regular on a summer series titled *Showcase 68* on NBC where she caught the attention of Nabors' producers.

To her credit, she performed at Caesar's Palace as the youngest opening act for Frank Sinatra, when she was sixteen years old. Sinatra was a role model for Julie Budd and she admittedly copied some of his style.

Budd performed the title song for the acclaimed 1972 film *Living Free* and her song "One Fine Day" reached 93 on the Billboard charts.

The cancellation of Jim's variety show did nothing to faze him. He and Ronnie headed for Vegas.

In the mid 2010s, getTV broadcast a few episodes of *The Jim Nabors Hour*. There were fervent hopes that the whole series might be seen after almost fifty years.

As far as any of our research indicates, those episodes may not even exist. Episodes known to have survived besides the opener are the ones with Kate Smith and Phyllis Diller.

Jim and Ronnie forever!

A sad fact of life is, some early and even not-so- early television programming is lost. If *The Jim Nabors Hour* ever is found and could be transferred to DVD for public release, it would be greeted with mass excitement by fans.

Variety shows were mostly a product of their time—costly to produce and made specifically for a certain audience. Some efforts to revive the genre in recent years have fallen flat.

Neil Patrick Harris found this out in 2015 when he hosted an elaborate revival of the variety show called *Best Time Ever*. It was a great idea on NBC's part and was broadcast live. It only aired for two months.

Jim Nabors had plenty of time left to further his singing career, but not so much his acting or comedy skills. His best work without a doubt can be found on *Gomer Pyle, U.S.M.C.*

However, his two-season variety show cannot be discounted. It was very important in the annals of television and his long career.

In this case, one could say, "They just don't make them like that anymore," and be 100 percent accurate.

(15)
POST-PYLE

Gomer Pyle, U.S.M.C. produced one hundred and fifty episodes, and like other sixties favorites, went straight from network to first-run syndication. It was so popular, CBS ran reruns during its daytime schedule for a while.

Back when daytime TV was worthy of watching, there were some series no longer on at night that dotted the network landscape. *All in the Family, Sanford and Son, The Jeffersons* (1975–1985), *Chico and the Man* (1974–1978), *Happy Days* (1974–1984), and *Alice* (1976–1985) are a few examples.

Then for most, it is rerun heaven, which means constant showings in regular syndication where shows are picked up for broadcast, usually in the order they were originally shown by affiliates.

The Gomer show was everywhere throughout the seventies and eighties. WTBS Atlanta kept it on for quite a while. There was a long gap of nearly thirty years or so that Gomer and gang mysteriously disappeared. The absence was long enough for an entire generation to not really gain any knowledge of the series.

We have spoken to young people who know the character Gomer Pyle from *The Andy Griffith Show*, but not from his own show. Our favorite Marine went AWOL through no fault of his own.

Perpetuating Private Pyle!

Thanks to MeTV, today a new generation is discovering *Gomer Pyle, U.S.M.C.* They have taken him to heart as much as we fans from the sixties did.

The more popular a series was during its original years, the more likely merchandise was made to cash in. There is a Gomer Pyle lunchbox, with many still around and in fairly good shape. There were comic books and even a novel by E. Kitzes Knox titled *Gomer Pyle* and released as a paperback by Pyramid in 1966.

The caricatures on the cover do not resemble either Jim Nabors or Frank Sutton. Not having read the novel, no other critique will be offered here.

As we wrap up this journey back to Camp Henderson, it seems fitting to hear from the many fans. They are quite vocal in their assessment of the show and have kept the enthusiasm very strong throughout this writing.

"Frank Sutton was a really good actor who died way too soon," writes John Michael Spell. "He and Jim Nabors had great chemistry together. I don't believe they were recognized enough for their work together. It is a good thing to keep the memory of their comedic teamwork alive."

Spell is a fan who met Jim Nabors at one of his live shows through a singer named Michael Rupert, who had been one of the singing Nabors kids on Jim's variety show.

Nabors was extremely nice and autographed one of his record albums.

The following reflections on *Gomer Pyle, U.S.M.C.* come from Craig Nystrom.

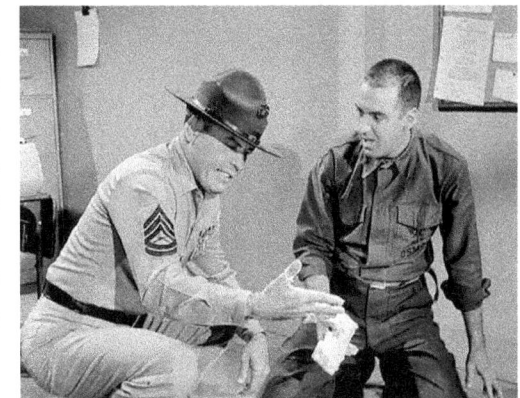

Frank Sutton and Jim Nabors— comedic chemistry in action.

"I grew up in a house without a television. I loved watching TV like all kids, but in order to do so I would need to go over to a friend's house or other family members' house to watch. When I would visit my grandparents' house each summer, my sister and I would pore over the *TV Guide* and plan what time we would get up in the morning and figure out what shows to watch.

"To this day I love all the classic TV shows from the 1960s: *The Beverly Hillbillies, Get Smart!, The Andy Griffith Show*, and of course, *Gomer Pyle, U.S.M.C.*

"Later, when I was in junior high school, I would walk or ride my bike over to my aunt and uncle's house three miles in the dark both ways to watch *The Dukes of Hazzard* (totally worth it!).

"During the 1970s, Jim Nabors was very popular. He was part of the concert series that would come to the local State fairgrounds every year. I lived a mile or so away, and on nights Jim Nabors was performing, I could hear him from my house. Keep in mind the only other sound I could hear from the fairgrounds was the fireworks.

"Over the years I quoted Jim any chance I could. "Surprise, Surprise, Surprise!," was probably my favorite line. "Goll-lee!" and "Shazam!" were also frequently used.

"Several episodes stand out in my mind. The episode involving Welsh rarebit, the poker game, and I have to include the episode where he sings "The Impossible Dream." If that song doesn't give you chills, you're not human.

"A few months ago I started watching the entire series in order. I checked the DVD set out of the local library and got to work watching. Like any show, many themes and situations were repeated. The key to the whole show is the Gomer and Carter interaction. Both actors were brilliant and had wonderful chemistry. Jim was the star, but he had to be willing to give screen time and even share the spotlight with Frank Sutton.

"Surprise, Surprise, Surprise!"

Generous Jim was more than willing to share the spotlight with Frank Sutton.

"Similar to Andy Griffith and Don Knotts, to name one example. I do think this show is as watchable today as ever; it holds up very well. Some of the dialogue and situations on the show would never make it on the air today, such as Aunt Bee insisting cleaning the barracks is woman's work. Overall, the show is very sweet and enjoyable.

"Watching it now brings back many wonderful memories for me and it will always be one of my favorite shows."

Oct. 24, 2018

Dave Monday mentioned that his favorite of the navy episodes is "Gomer Captures a Submarine" (Nov. 5, 1965).

The Marines are on a joint, amphibious mission with the navy when Gomer sinks a rubber raft with Carter and the others on it three times! Later, Carter makes him swim back to the ship in the ocean during heavy fog. On the way back, Gomer runs smack into an enemy submarine's periscope.

"Goll-lee, I done caught me a submarine!"

Dave also wondered at Lou Ann's naivete in her early episodes, because she seems to have no clue of Carter's real amorous intentions.

Randy Turner is a Mayberry scholar and author whom I called on frequently during the writing of this publication. In 2018, he published the Mayberry Day-by-Day

Gomer (Jim Nabors) seems to be the only one amused in the company of Colonel Gray (Forrest Compton) and guest star Tige Andrews in "Gomer Captures a Submarine."

Lou Ann's cluelessness makes Carter a nonstarter.

Flip Book Calendar. It is available along with other works of his at www.mayberrybooks.com.

He offered these reflections on *The Andy Griffith Show* episode titled "A Date for Gomer":

"Fillin' station attendant Gomer Pyle was introduced midway through the third season of *The Andy Griffith Show*, partially to fill the void left when Howard McNear, who played Floyd the barber, suffered a stroke. The inherent humor of the character of Gomer coupled with Jim Nabors' portrayal resulted in such popularity, Andy Griffith told story consultant Aaron Ruben that they needed to come up with a series featuring Gomer. Ruben, recognizing the success of an innocent country bumpkin placed in the officious and regimented world of the military in Andy Grifiith's previous portrayal of Will Stockdale in *No Time for Sergeants*, created the spin-off series *Gomer Pyle, U.S.M.C.*

From fillin' station to something more fulfillin.'

"By the time the episode 'A Date for Gomer' was filmed, the spin-off series was already planned. The episode was the tenth filmed during the fourth season of *The Andy Griffith Show*, though it was the ninth aired. The pilot episode 'Gomer Pyle, U.S.M.C.' was filmed but not aired until the final show of the season.

"In 'A Date for Gomer,' Barney and Thelma Lou are looking forward to the annual Chamber of Commerce dance, the biggest dance of the year. When Thelma Lou gets a call from her cousin, Mary Grace Gossage, she is elated that Mary Grace will be coming by to spend a few days with her but then realizes it will cause a problem. She insists Barney find a date for Mary Grace so she will not be left alone for the evening during the dance.

"Thelma Lou's cousin was played by Mary Grace Canfield, who is best remembered as the handywoman 'Ralph Monroe' on *Green Acres*. Barney shallowly judges Mary Grace on her looks alone, telling Thelma Lou her cousin is a dog. Eventually, he and Andy ask Gomer to accompany Mary Grace to the dance. Gomer agrees to go after repeatedly asking if she was pretty, to which they responded that she was 'nice.' Barney responds that Gomer has the same qualities, saying, 'You don't really know him, Thelma Lou. If you ever took the trouble to get underneath all that oil and gasoline smell, you'd find a heck of a human being.'

"Thelma Lou and Helen Crump, Andy's date, then have to convince Mary Grace to go to the dance with Gomer. She agrees after they assure her that they will be with her the entire time and after describing Gomer as 'tall, dark'—and just as Andy and Barney had done—'nice.'

"Gomer is clearly excited about the dance. He invested in a pair of new yellow socks which he worried might be too porous since he didn't want the hair on his legs to stick out. He bought a new purple tie with an acorn pattern and a new eight-dollar pair of shoes with brass buckles on the sides. He explains his financial investment by saying Mary Grace could be 'Miss Right.' Andy cautions Gomer not to over-expect.

"The three men arrive at Thelma Lou's house to pick up the women. When the plain Mary Grace comes into the room, the camera initially shows only Andy and Barney greeting her, saying it was nice to see her again, leaving the audience to wonder how

Gomer's initial reaction to meeting Mary Grace Gossage (played by Mary Grace Canfield) appeared to be positive, making it all the more mysterious when he ducked out shortly after.

Gomer is reacting to her plain appearance. He reacts with an almost childlike innocence. In a laugh-out-loud gesture, as the group haltingly makes small talk before leaving for the dance, Gomer tries to be suave by crossing his leg to be sure Mary Grace has a good look at his new socks and shoes. Gomer is then seen to look slightly worried. He

Gomer's new yellow socks pass the porosity test as Mary Grace looks on in considerable consternation.

abruptly stands up and asks to be excused, saying there is something he needs to do, and quickly leaves.

"Believing Gomer has dumped her, and having convinced the others go to the dance without her, Mary Grace is surprised when Gomer returns. He apologizes for taking so long, explaining he had to go to a couple of places to find something with a little pink in it to match her dress. Mary Grace says she doesn't understand, and Gomer explains he purchased a corsage (which he pronounced 'core-sage' with a long 'a') for her, since he realized Helen and Thelma Lou had one and she did not. He explains, 'It wouldn't be right for you, Mary Grace, to go to the dance unadorned.'

The sweet thoughtfulness of Gomer was evident when he returned with a corsage for Mary Grace, not wanting to see his date go "unadorned."

"Gomer and Mary Grace decide to stay at Thelma Lou's. When the others come back, they discover the couple enthusiastically dancing to blaring music. Gomer excuses himself and dances over to Andy and Barney, telling them happily they were right: 'She's nice! She's real nice!'

"Gomer's innate goodness and innocence are on full display in this wonderful episode. It would be difficult to watch 'A Date for Gomer' and not feel better about humanity. *The Andy Griffith Show* and *Gomer Pyle, U.S.M.C.* both excelled at showing that love and understanding were present in the human condition, even if it was not always readily apparent in 'the real world.'

"The shows were escapism but in the best sense of the word. 'A Date for Gomer' aired on November 25, 1963, just three days after the assassination of President John F. Kennedy. Throughout the rest of the decade, these series continued to offer respite from the nightly news filled with so much strife over issues such as the Vietnam War, protests, and the fight for civil rights and against racism in the United States. The world can still seem to often not realize the basic goodness at the core of humanity, which is one of the reasons these series still speak so perfectly to audiences many decades after they first aired."

Perhaps there are no more poignant memories of an episode than those of Terry Grundy who brought up "Little Girl Blue" (Feb. 4, 1966).

When everyone else returns from the dance to find Gomer and Mary Grace dancing up a storm, he announces to all just how "real nice" she really is!

The visiting colonel's lonely little daughter, Margaret, played by Christine Matchett.

It shows Gomer Pyle's true spirit and abiding kindness. He befriends the lonely daughter of a visiting colonel and almost ruins the big party.

Christine Matchett plays the little girl. As Margaret, neglected daughter of Colonel Matthews (Nelson Olmstead), she returns Gomer's lost button and they become fast friends.

Gomer teaches a good, clean, fun game you can play all by yourself!

In one scene, Gomer helps her figure out a game she can play by herself that won't dirty up her dress. They improvise a game of jacks using sugar cubes.

There are also tender scenes where Gomer looks through her photo album, they play records, and he sings "Put on a Happy Face." The song is possibly excised from some of the airings of this episode.

What "Little Girl Blue" does is show how Gomer thinks and acts with a child's innocence and sees the world through unbiased eyes.

There is plenty of humor, especially at the party, involving "avacader dip." We also have a stern governess named Miss Simms (Amzie Strickland) who later turned up as one of Bob Hartley's patients on *The Bob Newhart Show*.

The episode ends with a farewell game of jacks, and the moral seems to be: never interrupt a man when he's going for his "threesies."

As generations pass and times change, so too will tastes. We tend to think certain shows like *The Andy Griffith Show* and *Gomer Pyle, U.S.M.C.* are timeless and will continue to gain new audiences. This idea is proving to

Gomer pays rapt attention to his new little friend, making her feel important and loved.

ring true. Young people are increasingly discovering the classics, and with no preconceived notions, are finding them funny.

Ronnie Schell carries the torch for Gomer Pyle. The same can be said for a style of comedy that is clean and hilarious, a style he helped popularize. His legacy and work will live on. To this day, he maintains a hearty schedule of attending events and meeting and greeting fans.

Let me share with you an event that happened at a home in Calhoun, Georgia in the summer of 2018. Ronnie and I sat at a kitchen table discussing stories of Hollywood, past and present. *Gomer Pyle, U.S.M.C.* played on the television courtesy of the DVD set. The room was full of people who had come to see Ronnie the night before he was to do his *Tribute to Jim Nabors* the next night in the town's historic theater.

"How's about a chip and some avacader dip?"

A young boy of possibly eleven was glued to the television set. A scene came on with a close-up of Ronnie Schell. I told him directly, "You see that guy on TV? That's him sitting over there."

He got up from the couch, walked over to the kitchen table, looked at Ronnie, then back at the TV screen.

"It *is* him!" he yelled excitedly.

It has been an extreme pleasure bringing this book, a labor of love, to completion. On behalf of everyone at Camp Henderson, we salute you! May your days be filled with laughter and your worries few. Catch a rerun whenever you can. Return to the good old days if only for thirty minutes at a time. You will be glad you did.

Dismissed.

www.ingramcontent.com/pod-product-compliance
Lightning Source LLC
Chambersburg PA
CBHW050113170426
43198CB00014B/2555